Captain
Two Voices

Disclaimer

My accounts of events are all written from a personal perspective, as I recollect them; it spans the years from 1989 until 2021, and is based on the entries in my pilot's log book.

Some readers may recall events differently, but we all have our own perspective on life and that's what makes us human. So please forgive any discrepancies. It has never been my intention to offend or upset anyone; in fact, quite the opposite, my objective has been simply to write an honest, informative and entertaining account of my flying life.

Les Homewood   January 2021

Captain Two Voices

The Memoirs of a Private Pilot

LES HOMEWOOD

THE CHOIR PRESS

First published in the United Kingdom in 2022 by
The Choir Press

ISBN 978-1-78963-303-0

For my family and friends
that have flown with me, and trusted me
to get them safely back down on the ground,
and my daughter Katie, who has not flown with me,
but always listens to my anecdotes.

Also, for my instructors and examiners,
without whom I would not have been able to fly.

Contents

1

Introduction

'Flying might not be all smooth sailing,
but the fun of it is worth the price.'

AMELIA EARHART

How It All Began

All my life, from a small boy, I have been fascinated by the aeroplanes in the sky above me, by the thought of flight in general, and the science behind it.

There is some old cinefilm my dad took of me when I was about three years old. We were in my grandfather's garden in Welling. I heard a loud noise overhead and looked up to see three Gloster Meteor Jet Fighters flying in formation. Little did I know then, whilst being filmed, that not only would I be able to travel as a passenger in large planes to distant countries across the world, but would myself one day learn to fly; not jet fighters but light aircraft. Flying would become my hobby for thirty years and counting.

My education was certainly no more than average, and at the time when I was leaving school, socio-demographics usually determined one's future. Boys and girls would frequently follow in their respective fathers' and mothers' footsteps when it came to looking for employment and choosing careers.

My father worked for the General Post Office, usually called the GPO, driving parcel delivery vans from a depot in Union Street, near London Bridge. On many occasions I went to work with him, mainly at weekends, where I would play among the wheeled, wicker-sided parcel bins. I am pleased to say I never followed my dad into the GPO; if I had done so, I don't suppose I would have had the wherewithal to be able to afford lessons to qualify and hold a private pilot's licence (PPL), and to enjoy flying many types of light aircraft.

Now, at sixty-nine years old, I have retired from running a company with my business partner, and long-time friend, Stan Wright. We started a company in 1976, when we were both very young men, with ambition and self-belief, certain that all would be good in our world, forever. We had been mates, working 'on the tools' as thermal insulation engineers, or laggers, since 1971. To this day we have total faith and trust in one another, which I suppose is why, as fifty-fifty business partners, we finally sold our company in 2018, still as fifty-fifty business partners. Many marriages do not last as long as the business relationship we've had, and still have.

Ironically, whilst visiting a site at Biggin Hill during 1978, I wanted to find out about flying light aircraft. One of our previous bosses, Dennis Ballard, who influenced and mentored both of us, had started taking flying lessons at Biggin Hill. Out of curiosity, we called into the flying club on the airfield. Some years later, this flying club was to become a significant part of my life, as you will discover.

In the early days of our business, our wives used to joke that they wouldn't be surprised if we two moved in together. We were that close, and worked such long hours together, to build our business. The relationship Stan and I had was strong and fraternal. We frequently played practical jokes on each other, often criticised one another, but we would always stand together in a crisis.

Now, fast forward to 1989. Stan and I were well known in our industry, and were often invited to corporate events. Apart from the social aspect, which we both enjoyed, they provided us with an opportunity to meet our competitors and promote our company.

On this particular occasion we had been invited to one such event at the Biggin Hill Air Fair in June 1989. There was a free bar and the usual sort of corporate catering. Before long, *The Boys*, as we were known by some of our competitors, were working the room and enjoying the event. Our hosts, the sales reps employed by the multinational supplier footing the bill for the event, were being lazy, apparently uninterested in entertaining any of their guests, and making little effort to schmooze with their clients. We were making contacts and promoting our company. If you could pull that one off, why wouldn't you?

Towards the end of that gloriously warm and sunny afternoon, we clambered into a coach to carry us across the airfield at Biggin Hill, so we could visit the merchandising stands, information displays, shops and the large funfair provided to entertain the tens of thousands of air show visitors.

Stan and I were really enjoying the day, not only watching the aircraft displays, but also looking around the many and varied merchandise stands set out on this colossal World War Two airfield.

We somehow lost each other for an hour or so. I think I stopped to look at some military exhibits, and Stan kept walking. Eventually we bumped into each other again and Stan thrust a small piece of crumpled paper in my hand.

With the portentous words, 'Don't say I never buy you anything,' Stan laughed, and recounted the following story to me:

Not long after we lost sight of each other, I was walking around, and there was this little aeroplane with a booth next to it, and a young-looking man, sitting there looking very bored. I stopped to ask him what was the reason for him and the aeroplane being there.

The young man became energised, and spoke almost without drawing breath for about twenty minutes, telling me all about the amazing feeling of freedom and fun you experience when you have a private pilot's licence, and how you can fly from Biggin Hill to Le Touquet in France for lunch. He continued to describe, in great detail, what was involved in the process of getting a PPL.

Anyway, when he eventually ran out of adjectives to describe the awesome experiences you can have flying light aircraft, he asked me if I would like to buy a trial flying lesson to experience this for myself, and maybe continue to become a private pilot. I smiled at him and told him that I would buy a trial lesson.

He looked positively ecstatic, and so pleased with himself that he had managed to sell a £75 voucher for a trial flying lesson. He asked me the name to be put on the voucher, so I told him: L R Homewood.

He wrote your name on the gift voucher, then got out the swipe machine and I handed him my credit card.

He looked at the card for a few seconds, then looked up at me a bit confused and said suspiciously, 'You gave me the name L R Homewood for the gift voucher, but this card says S W Wright ...'

I replied, 'That's right. If you think you would get me up in one of those bloody things, you can think again. It looks like a good fart would blow it over. I've bought this for my friend Les, to frighten the shit out of him.'

He shrugged his shoulders, swiped the card, took the slip from the machine, peeled off my copy and gave me the gift voucher.

When Stan finished talking, I carefully flattened the crumpled piece of paper, and read with growing anticipation the words *Trial Flying Lesson for L R Homewood*. The flying school and club that had sold Stan the lesson was based at Biggin Hill and traded as King Air. I later discovered that King Air was run by Margaret and Vince Butler. Margaret was the chief flying instructor (CFI). A day or two later, I contacted King Air and arranged a date for my trial lesson.

I turned up at Biggin Hill, and reported to reception at the King Air office. I was given a briefing about what to expect. Then, I was escorted by an instructor to a Cessna 152 sitting on the apron, outside the flying club. I can't recall his name, but it was his job to take me out for my first-ever flight in a light aircraft and give me a trial flying lesson.

We took off from runway 03 at Biggin Hill, and headed towards Wrotham. Once in the air, with the aircraft trimmed for straight and level flight by the instructor, I was given the opportunity to take control of the aircraft. I must say, it felt really good. Flying seemed to be natural and instinctive. I knew immediately this was something for me.

When it came to carrying out a turn, I asked without any prompting, 'Do I press on the left rudder when carrying out a left-hand turn?'

The instructor confirmed that this was correct. He then explained the effects of the rudder input. I knew then that this was not going to be a one-off jolly. I was getting hooked.

On the return to Biggin Hill, after about forty minutes, the instructor took control. We were over Knatts Valley near Brands Hatch; almost overhead our company premises. He put the aircraft into a dive, then pulled up straight, just before the plane stalled, performing what I know now was a knife-edge stall turn. This, combined with a steep turn on to finals, prior to landing on runway 29 back at Biggin Hill, had entirely the opposite of the effect Stan had anticipated.

It had been a fantastic experience, and I was confident that I would enjoy the physical and mental challenge of learning to fly. Once we had landed, I stepped out of the aeroplane, grinning from ear to ear, and told the instructor, 'This is the hobby for me.'

So, let the following pages be a friendly warning to anyone reading them. Having a trial flying lesson could enrich your life forever, whilst simultaneously depleting your bank balance. Flying is not a cheap pastime, but I can't think of another that will give you as much pleasure, exhilaration and the privilege of looking down at the Earth from 1500 hundred feet.

You don't have to be an astronaut to look down in wonder at our planet. From a small aircraft you can observe sheep being rounded up by a working dog; cattle and ponies quietly grazing; centuries-old castles and cathedrals; roads, rivers and railways snaking across the countryside; the shadow cast by your own plane on the downland pasture below; the seasonally changing colours of patchwork fields and woodlands, or your own village and home from an aerial perspective.

Every flight brings new delights. Even more breath-taking, if you start to learn aerobatics, is the first time you see the ground rushing up towards you, as you look through the plexiglass roof of a Cessna 152 Aerobat from the top of a loop.

I hope you will find the following pages interesting, maybe instructive or thought-provoking, but most of all entertaining.

2

Flying Training
Getting a PPL

'When once you have tasted flight, you will forever walk the earth
with your eyes turned skyward, for there you have been,
and there you will always long to return.'

LEONARDO DA VINCI

Onward and Upward

I turned up at the King Air office at Biggin Hill at around 11:30 on the 11th July 1989. After introductions, my instructor Mike Clayton booked out a Cessna 152, call sign G BIOM, Golf Bravo India Oscar Mike. You must learn the International Radiotelephony Spelling Alphabet, also known as the NATO Phonetic Alphabet, pretty quickly. Other pilots and air traffic controllers need to know who you are, be it on the ground or in the air. Imagine the confusion if everyone made up their own spelling alphabets to communicate? You could say Bertie, Billy, Biggles or Brandy for the letter B.

So now the time had come. We were standing next to a two-seat Cessna 152 training and touring aircraft. In common with most flying schools, these aircraft were not in their first flush of youth. However, this did not deter me. All I wanted to do was get into the air again and feel the exhilaration of cheating gravity, losing contact with the ground and becoming airborne.

We commenced a check-out of the external surfaces of the aircraft. It required the agility of a mountain goat to climb on to the foothold of the wing spar in order to access the fuel filler cap on each wing and establish the quantity of fuel in the tanks for our forthcoming flight, and my first lesson.

The first lesson, prescribed by the syllabus, covers the basic skills needed to safely operate a heavier-than-air flying machine. Mike was at the controls for the first take-off, explaining the control of the aircraft, via the yoke, which is similar to the steering wheel in a car.

As soon as we were in the air and out of the Biggin circuit, Mike spoke the words I was waiting to hear, 'You have control.'

I could hardly believe that the lad who had left school at fifteen years of age, without a single qualification other than bronze and silver medals for personal survival in a swimming pool, dressed in pyjamas, was now embarking on a course of practical and theoretical training and examination to become a pilot.

Taking control of that Cessna 152 was incredible. Even after thirty-one years of flying, I still remember the sheer elation of that moment. Next came instruction in trimming the aircraft. No, not with scissors, but by adjusting the tabs on the elevator. The result, when the aircraft is trimmed correctly, is like exchanging an older car without power steering for a brand-new model.

The following hour went by in a flash, from take-off to the landing, which was also carried out by my instructor. I could not believe how quickly the time had flown.

Back on the ground, we had a debriefing, and discussed the next part of my flying training and what I could expect. My instructor was calm and knowledgeable. I had confidence in him and I knew I wanted to become a pilot. To say I was elated at the prospect of what lay ahead was the understatement of the year. Straight away, I purchased my pilot's log book from the flying shop at Biggin Hill. In the log book would be recorded the dates and times of every flight, and my progress towards gaining my private pilot's licence (PPL). Each element of my instruction, each manoeuvre and exercise I completed, had to be recorded in the log book, and signed off by the instructor.

When our debrief was completed, I had to deal with the reality of the lesson; the payment. As far as I can recall, the cost of each lesson was between ninety-five pounds and one hundred and ten pounds for an hour. Back in 1989, that was not an insignificant amount of money. You could by a pint of bitter for around ninety pence, and a litre of petrol for thirty-nine pence. So, you can imagine, at around a hundred pounds for an hour's flying, inclusive of instruction, this was not the cheapest hobby I could have taken up. Not if you compare it with fishing, playing football, or stamp collecting, all of which, oddly enough, I had tried at some time during my life, and was not really hooked by any of those pastimes. I arranged my second lesson for 17th July; I was determined this was the hobby for me, so I had no time to waste.

I left King Air, and drove back to my office in West Kingsdown, re-living in my mind what I had just done. I must have bored everyone in the office with retelling what had happened during that first lesson.

However, my wife was blissfully unaware that I had taken my first flying lesson. When I arrived home that evening, I explained what had happened that day. I showed her the log book, and told her that I intended to complete the course, and gain my private pilot's licence. She looked and sounded quite shocked.

She responded, 'So when is the next lesson booked for? Next month?'

There was a look of surprise and disbelief when I said, 'No, I've booked another lesson for next week, and I intend to be qualified as quickly as I can.'

Maybe it is selective amnesia, but I can't remember exactly what she said next. Probably that's just as well. I guess there can't have been too much of a domestic incident, as I have now been qualified for more than thirty-one years. Nothing was going to prevent me from continuing with my flying training, and nothing did. I qualified less than four months later.

My second lesson couldn't come soon enough. I had purchased the Trevor Thom publications, from *Air Pilot's Manual 1 Flying Training* to *Air Pilot's Manual 5 Radio Navigation and Instrument Flying*. These standard works were recommended by my instructor Mike Clayton. Ahead of my next lesson, I pored over each exercise with a real fervour. I had an almost obsessive desire to learn as much as I could, and to become a pilot as quickly as possible.

For the second lesson, we booked out the aircraft Oscar Mike again and proceeded to the apron to complete the pre-flight checks. These essential safety and fuel checks are carried out by the pilot-in-charge before every flight in any aircraft, small or large. At least, that's what is supposed to happen.

It is far better to find out on the ground that the locking nut on one of the flaps is missing before you have left the ground, rather than taking to the air, then realising that one flap won't extend because it's disconnected from the control mechanism.

If there is only enough fuel in the tanks to get you up to 1500 feet, followed by an ominous silence when the engine stops, there is only one direction you and the aeroplane are going, as gravity takes control of your destiny.

Pre-flight checks all completed, we departed Biggin as we had done a week earlier. Up into the blue we went. However, as we flew over Kent, Mike informed me that he was leaving King Air. An opening for him to join a commercial airline academy had come up, which was an offer he couldn't refuse. Subsequently, I found out that many of the instructors working in flying clubs up and down the UK are transitory. Instructing is their stepping stone to the left-hand seat of the passenger jet that takes the likes of you and me on holiday, or on business trips around the globe. This was Mike's chance to realise his dream. I listened to his news intently, and for a moment imagined myself in that jet airliner left-hand seat.

But I was a fifty-fifty director-owner of my company, now in its thirteenth year of trading under the name SL, obviously a combination of my first initial with that of my business partner Stan. We were reasonably successful. At this time, I was driving my pride and joy, a white Porsche 911 Carrera Targa. So, I stopped pipe-dreaming, congratulated Mike, and asked him who would be teaching me after his departure from King Air, which was imminent.

He said, 'I've asked Margaret Butler to continue with your flying training,' and went on to explain that she was not only an experienced pilot and an excellent instructor, but also the chief flying instructor (CFI) and co-owner of King Air.

To be honest, in 1989, although we had a female prime minister, the times were not as enlightened. There were far fewer career opportunities for women than in 2021. I didn't realise there were female flying instructors, so I just hoped that being Margaret Butler's student was going to be a positive experience.

On 21st July, the day of my third lesson, I was introduced to Margaret by Janey, the friendly receptionist, and general go-to for all things administrative at King Air.

Janey said to Margaret, 'This is Les Homewood, Mike was teaching him.'

Margaret had an almost-scarily, cool demeanour. I could tell that she was a serious teacher, and I would have to work hard on my practical training, as well as preparing for the desk-based exams, which are part of the syllabus.

As before, we took the keys of a Cessna 152. This time we were flying G BLZH. Every plane is registered with a unique identifier or registration mark, which is displayed on the side of the fuselage and doubles as a call sign. In most countries, unscheduled general aviation flights identify themselves using the call sign corresponding to the aircraft's registration mark. G indicates it is a UK registered aircraft. In our case, the Cessna 152 call sign had to be given as '*Golf Bravo Lima Zulu Hotel*' when initially communicating with the tower, but was then abbreviated in following messages, to '*Zulu Hotel*.'

After the pre-flight checks were completed, I climbed into my usual student seat, the pilot's seat on the left-hand side of the cockpit, and for the first time, under Margaret's supervision I took off from Biggin, and climbed away from the airfield.

We were heading towards the Isle of Grain, the eastern part of the Hoo Peninsula. At that time, it was a good area for PPL students to train. It is sparsely populated, with a few isolated farmhouses, shabby agricultural buildings and the remnants of wartime defences. The area was ideal for us novice pilots to learn and practice our skills. Mainly, there were sheep grazing on the marshes and fields below, with Southend Airport well away to the east, so we had the sky to ourselves.

In the main, Margaret would show me a manoeuvre, explaining what she was doing at the time, and why. Then I would carry out some repeat manoeuvres. As I said before, I felt instinctively that I could fly. These exercises were ticked off from the syllabus that Margaret and all instructors have to work to. Quite quickly, I learnt to make climbing turns, descending turns, and trim the aircraft during flight.

I do enjoy the fact that the pilot in control of even the smallest light aircraft, has the courtesy title of captain. I laugh now at my bravado, the confidence or maybe arrogance of my thirty-eight-year-old self. However, the area of my training that really did test my nerve, was carrying out stalls, and the recovery from a stall. Obviously, it is preferable not to let the aircraft you are flying get into a stall in the first place, thereby rendering the knowledge of '*recovery from a stall*' unnecessary. However, you and I know that, in real life, anything can happen at any time, even to the most experienced of pilots. Therefore, the skill of stall recovery is essential to learn and to practise.

So, Margaret explained the manoeuvre we were about to perform. The way she described what was about to happen made me not so much apprehensive as bloody terrified. Margaret climbed Zulu Hotel up to about 2400 feet, eased the power off, to not much more than a tick over, then gradually pulled the control yoke back. This caused the nose of ZH to search for outer space, which is what it felt like, as we were sitting there, looking up into the blue yonder.

This procedure was soon followed by a screeching sound coming from the audible stall warner. This was followed shortly by a shaking and buffeting of the wings, as the airflow over the upper surface of the wings decreased. This resulted in Margaret, Zulu Hotel and me suddenly exchanging our view of the stratosphere for a view of terra firma. Gravity was beckoning us down towards the grazing sheep, who were unaware of our rapid descent to Mother Earth. That first stall was a real eye-opener and wake-up call to the serious nature of the hobby I was pursuing. Was this really going to be a skill I could master?

After we had completed all of the height and safety checks prior to stall practise, it was inevitably my turn.

Margaret said, 'Now it's your turn! You saw what I did. Reduce power back to just above idle. Keep pulling the controls back, listen for the stall warner, wait for the buffeting of the wings, then as the aircraft loses lift, and the nose drops, give it full power. Centre the wings with the appropriate rudder input, and pull up out of the dive to straight and level. Apply cruise power as we achieve straight and level again. OK?'

I felt like saying, 'No. I'm not ready for this,' but obviously that was not an option if I was to achieve my PPL.

So, there we were, just on the edge of Hoo, near the Thames, at 2400 feet or so. I started the syllabus exercise *Stalls and Recovery*, just as Margaret had shown me. Reduce power – check. Pull back on the controls, lifting the nose of the aircraft – check. I can now hear the stall warner screaming in my ears like a banshee – check. Wings are now buffeting like a pigeon trying to take off in a hurricane – check. The nose of ZH dropped like a stone, and in an instant, all I could see was good old Father Thames directly in front of us, as we were now in a vertical dive towards the briny.

In fright, I threw my arms out sideways, exclaiming, 'Jeeeez!'

Margaret immediately took over control of ZH, recovering the aircraft to straight and level.

She then said, 'Maybe a little less forward on the controls next time, Les. I wasn't expecting to go swimming in the Thames today, or I would have brought my swimming costume with me.'

We climbed back up to a good height, and started the whole manoeuvre again. This time I was a bit less forceful on the forward control, and recovered the aircraft without losing too much height, and ruining either mine or Margaret's underwear in the process. So, that was lesson three completed.

After every lesson, there was a thorough debriefing, during which I took on board every suggestion and criticism Margaret made in order to help me qualify and be the best pilot I could be.

As I mentioned before, there are also written exams – this was the format in the days before digital exams on a computer screen. Margaret told me that students taking their first exams, such as air law, usually achieve a higher pass mark than they do in subsequent exams, because it is all still a novelty. The desire to be a qualified pilot is all consuming, and the most important thing on your mind, so more effort goes into the preparation for the first exams.

She was not wrong. My passion, in common with most students, was all about the flying. I knew I had to pass all the written exams, but any time spent on the ground studying, I saw as an interruption. I wanted to progress as quickly as I could to getting my backside in the captain's seat, in sole charge of an aeroplane.

Before I would be allowed to fly solo, I had to pass the air law exam. Air law covers the sort of dos and don'ts of aviation such as the minimum heights at which you are allowed to fly above people and buildings in different areas. The regulations vary depending whether you are flying over the countryside, over a built-up housing area, or above sensitive sites such as power stations, prisons or other airfields.

I also had to obtain a radio telephony licence (RT). As a private pilot you have to use the correct terminology for communication between the aircraft and control tower, or other aircraft. Which meant I had to acquire the rising and falling intonation of speech that you hear from an airline pilot, when you are flying off to sunny climes on holiday. More about Captain Two Voices a bit later.

The RT exam was carried out in the club building. I was shut into a room with a small desk, and a headset, while the RT instructor was in another room, also wearing a headset. I had to simulate the communication between the pilot (me) and the air traffic controller (Instructor George, another rather scary character, small of stature, but to a novice PPL student quite intimidating).

With both the RT and air law exams under my belt I was feeling positive; the minimum pass mark for air law was 60%, and I had achieved 98%. However, my marks did drop somewhat in the later exams, as Margaret had predicted. All I wanted to do was walk out of the air side of the club building and go flying. I did pass all my exams without any re-takes, although the last ones were, to be honest, a scrape through.

All I needed now was a Class 2 medical. This is something you can only obtain from an aviation medical examiner (AME). There are so many abbreviations for everything connected with aviation, I was discovering. My AME worked for the RAF, examining fast jet pilots and the like, as well as dealing with the PPL requirement down at the bottom end of the aviation scale. I obtained my medical without any problems. I had hoped that would be the case, as I was a fit, healthy and active thirty-eight years old then.

Going Solo

After a further five lessons, between 26th July and 17th August, I had passed all the relevant exams and a medical, which would allow me to fly solo. As we were approaching Biggin Hill, at the end of my eighth lesson – yet another fantastically rewarding session – Margaret told me that she felt the time was right for my next lesson to include my first solo flight!

We had spoken about this stage of my flight training at times during previous lessons. When you are facing the prospect of being up in the air, in sole charge of an aircraft, without the comfort of an instructor sitting beside you with her thousands of hours of experience, the level of anticipation and concentration increases tenfold. I had been longing for this moment. I was sure I was capable of flying the aircraft on my own because my confidence was growing all the time.

During the earlier years of the Second World War, pilots would be sent off to fly solo with as little as five hours instruction in a de Havilland Tiger Moth. Pilots and other aircrew were so desperately needed to fight the German Luftwaffe, bomb enemy territory, and avoid Britain falling into enemy hands, that Britain and its allies established the single largest aviation training programme in history, the British Commonwealth Air Training Plan.

Fortunately for me, there was no war in Europe in 1989, so the need for me to fly solo did not have the same imperative. However, Margaret did have a reputation for getting her students ready to fly solo soon after they had completed the minimum number of hours required at that time. In 1989 the minimum was ten hours before you can attempt a solo flight. By now, yours truly had a grand total of ten hours and five minutes flying training under my belt, and recorded in my log book. I was quite pleased that Margaret felt I was now ready to go solo.

* * *

Before I go any further, let me explain about the name *Captain Two Voices*. At the time of my flying training, during 1989, my family lived in the village of East Farleigh, in Kent. When we moved there, we made friends with a couple whom I met one evening in a local pub, the Walnut Tree. Alison and Malcolm Chatterley were quite a bit younger than us, but we had a great time together, irrespective of the age gap. We would go out to dinner with Alison and Malcolm about once a fortnight. As they were both local, and knew the area, they invariably chose the establishment we would visit.

There was a pub called the Provender in another Kentish village, Ulcombe. The Provender was run by a former semi-professional comedian by the name of Martin. I don't think I ever knew his surname.

One evening we went with Ali and Malc to the Provender for the first time. The restaurant served succulent lasagnes, which were a garlic lover's delight.

Jean and I were introduced to Martin, who trotted out his banter from his club days, which was quite funny. At least, the first time you heard his gags it was quite funny.

Martin came over to take our order. Whilst standing at our table he said to me, 'Don't I know you, Les?'

I knew I had never seen him before, so replied, 'No, you must be mistaking me for somebody else.'

He shrugged, and walked off to serve other diners. A short while later he stopped to talk to Malcolm and Alison, who were old friends of his, glanced at me and said again, 'I'm sure I know you, Les.'

Again, I said, 'I don't think so, I'm sure I would remember you, if we had met before.'

Martin looked perplexed and walked away. He deserved an Oscar for this. He returned with our food.

As we were about to tuck in, he ventured, 'I think I've got it. Les, do you fly aeroplanes?'

This was the hook going right through my lip, like a fly fisherman catching a prize salmon on the River Dee.

I replied, in a voice that maybe others in the restaurant could hear too, 'Yes, I do actually, I am training to get a private pilot's licence.'

'That's it. I knew it,' he said. 'I work part-time as an air traffic controller in the control tower at Biggin Hill Airport. Don't you sometimes fly a Cessna 152, call sign Golf Bravo Oscar Yankee Alpha?'

'Yes ...' I responded, believing his story whilst thinking, 'How else would he know the call sign of the plane that I flew quite regularly?'

'Do you know what we call you when you approach the airfield?'

'No ...' I replied, still believing every word he was saying.

'We call you Captain Two Voices, and we roll about laughing on the floor of the control tower as you are talking to us.' Martin delivered his punchline.

Alison, Malcolm, and my wife were, by now, crying with laughter. Then the penny dropped. I had been set up. Jean had been passing on information to Alison about the aircraft I was flying, and various other nuggets. She, in turn, passed it on to Martin, just enough for him to make up a plausible story and reel me in. This had been going on for some time. I must confess, it still makes me laugh, thirty-one years later, and I have never lost the name *Captain Two Voices.*

My Captain's Voice is different from my Normal Voice. In common with most pilots and ATCs, my speech when using radio communication needs to be slower, with short sentences and some standard phrases. Pronunciation is more deliberate, with lots of rising and falling intonation, which makes speech easier to understand. As soon as I climb inside the plane I code-switch into my 'Captain Two Voices' voice.

* * *

Back to the flying. It was the afternoon of 22nd August 1989. Margaret and I departed from Biggin Hill in the best trainer on their fleet, a Cessna 152 Aerobat, Golf Bravo Oscar Yankee Alpha. As the name suggests, it was an aeroplane built to be able to cope with the stresses of g-force experienced when carrying out aerobatic manoeuvres. Aerobatics require some serious grunt and Yankee Alpha certainly had that in spades.

G-BOYA, or Yankee Alpha, by comparison with the average 152 training aircraft, was a bit of an aerial sports car. Yet, at the same time, it was tolerant and accepting of a novice pilot's actions when flying.

We left Biggin around 17:20 and flew south to Redhill Aerodrome in Surrey. Redhill is a grass runway airfield, with the M23 to the east; Gatwick Airport only a few miles to the south; a railway line, and East Surrey Hospital to the west; and the ridge of the North Downs to the north.

Fortunately, there is also a large indoor tennis complex on final approach to Redhill's runway 26, just west of the M23. The building has large translucent panels in the roof, which resemble the missing front teeth in a seven-year old's smile. This landmark is a great help to a new flying student, when Redhill is not your home aerodrome, and most of the local topography is green fields.

We did several circuits and bumps. This is an exercise in which you take off from the airfield, carry out a rectangular circuit of the aerodrome, approach and land on the same runway, then apply full power whilst rolling along the runway, and take off again. Then you repeat this exercise, thereby gaining experience of take-offs and landings, which are often the most challenging aspect of flying.

After the circuits, which I remember as if it were yesterday, Margaret told me to taxi to the control tower, which I duly did.

Margaret then gave me one last briefing, advising me emphatically, 'And at all costs, don't lose sight of Redhill Aerodrome whilst up in the air.'

With Yankee Alpha's engine still ticking over, Margaret got out of the plane, looked at me with a beaming smile, and said, 'You will find the plane will react a bit differently once my great lump is out of it. At all costs, don't lose sight of Redhill ...'

She was certainly not overweight, but I knew what she meant. The less weight in an aeroplane, the faster it accelerates, and subsequently ascends into the sky, where it is meant to be.

She also said, 'Good luck. You'll be fine. See you soon.'

Those words of encouragement did help me to retain my composure. I needed to concentrate calmly on what I was sure I could do, now it was going to be for real. Alone, I would be captain-in-charge of an aeroplane, flying at 1000 feet above the ground. Alone, I hoped to return the plane to the runway, rolling along on three wheels.

I taxied away, and noticed Margaret going into the control tower, not looking back at me in G-BOYA. A bit like a mother leaving her three-year-old at a nursery for the first time, I suppose. I did not have any self-doubts though.

In my best radio voice, I spoke to the tower, and informed them that I was G-BOYA, requesting departure information for a circuit. I was given clearance to taxi to the hold for runway 26.

The hold is an area defined by two white lines, a metaphoric barrier at the edge of the live runway, which you are not allowed across until given permission by the tower. After trundling along the taxi way, I reached the hold for runway 26, and carried out my power checks.

Again, I called up the tower and said, 'Golf Yankee Alpha at the hold for 26, ready for departure for one circuit.' The call sign I used was abbreviated. We had already completed several circuits, so they knew who we were.

Once given clearance for take-off, I took a deep breath, slowly pushed the throttle forward, enough to move G-BOYA from the hold and on to the active runway. I stopped briefly on the numbers to ensure the nose wheel was facing straight down the runway. If you don't ensure the nose wheel is straight when applying full power, you could start to veer off to one side of the runway, risking colliding with a light, or anything else that may be around.

Yankee Alpha and I steadily increased speed along the bumpy grass runway. Somewhere around forty-five or fifty knots indicated air speed I steadily pulled back on the controls, and in an instant, all the noise and vibration of rumbling over the less-than-billiard-table-flat grass ceased. All was smooth and quiet and calm, as we continued to climb out towards East Surrey Hospital.

I usually say *we*, even when it is only me flying. The pilot and the plane are a partnership. Les Homewood and his steed, G-BOYA. On passing overhead the hospital, at 500 feet or so, I continued to climb out, by now quite rapidly, and at the same time turning north towards the Downs, and upwards to 1000 feet above the airfield ground level, known as QFE.

Still ringing in my ears were Margaret's instructions, as she got out of the plane, 'And at all costs, don't lose sight of Redhill ...'

So, I kept a close eye, every few seconds, on the large expanse of green, with many aircraft hangars and parked aircraft dotted around the perimeter. I levelled off at 1000 feet, and turned to the east, the downwind leg of the circuit.

Now over the Downs, when I looked south, towards Redhill Airfield, I could see Gatwick, a few miles further to the south. I certainly did not want to get involved with their traffic, large jets approaching the airport with holiday makers and business people on board.

I made a radio call to the tower and announced that I was established downwind. The tower responded, telling me to report on final approach for runway 26.

Soon I was turning to the south, on to the base leg of the circuit, and flying parallel to the M23. This was a useful landmark too, as it guides you back towards the airfield.

Approaching the end of the base leg of the Redhill circuit, I completed my BUMFICHH checks, which must always be done before attempting a landing.

This acronym is used by pilots to ensure each element is checked prior to landing:

B = Brakes, off.
U = Undercarriage, this is fixed down on a 152.
M = Mixture, fuel mixture fully rich.
F = Fuel.
I = Instruments, check all instruments are correctly set.
C = Carb heat, engage carburettor heat to prevent ice build-up in carburettor venturi at slow speeds.
H + H = Hatches and Harnesses, doors secured and seat belts secure.

I had reduced my speed and height, engaged landing flaps, then proceeded to turn on to the final approach. I could now see the tennis centre, like a beacon encouraging me back to that lush, green airfield in Surrey. I called the tower again, and said, 'Golf Yankee Alpha, on finals to land.'

The reply was immediate, 'Golf Yankee Alpha, cleared to land, runway 26.'

They would have given me the wind direction and speed, but my memory is not so good that I can record the detail in this book. The sight of the runway getting ever closer was just amazing. I had nearly done it, only about half a mile to fly. Then, hopefully, to land G-BOYA with all three wheels going around.

I kept checking. Speed, attitude, speed, attitude. Now we were over the white-painted number 26 on the threshold of the runway, twenty feet or so from the ground. I pulled off all the remaining power, concentrating on the runway in front of me, continuing to maintain back pressure on the controls to prevent the nose wheel from landing first. We were gradually sinking, getting closer and closer to the runway. All of a sudden, the wheels of Yankee Alpha touched the grass. I had done it. I had taken off, completed a circuit away from the field, and returned. We were rolling along the bumpy runway, and the speed was reducing.

Then, a reassuring voice from the control tower said, 'Congratulations, Yankee Alpha, on your first solo.'

After leaving the active runway, I taxied back to the control tower again to collect my instructor.

Margaret climbed back into the right-hand seat of G-BOYA and said, 'Well done, Les. I was watching from the tower. It was a good take-off, and a good approach and landing. I'll fly back to Biggin. You'll be feeling so high, it'll be safer for me to fly.'

I could see where she was coming from. I think I could have taken on a crack team from the SAS at that moment. I know it took several days, if not weeks, for the smile to leave my face. A few days later, I was presented with my first solo certificate.

Know Where You Are Going

Next on the list of tasks to master from the syllabus are navigation and some limited instrument training. And more solo flying.

After going solo, the next lesson is used to carry out circuits with an instructor before there can be further solo flights. This is to ensure your skill and confidence are in the right proportions, and the instructor is happy for you to continue to build up the solo requirement of the PPL syllabus.

I turned up at Biggin Hill in the late morning of 24th August 1989, for my next lesson after my solo flight. When I booked in, I was told that Margaret was not in that day, and that her husband Vince Butler was to be my temporary instructor. I was introduced to Vince, who on first meeting didn't seem too friendly!

I was instructed, as usual, to go to the aircraft first to start the pre-flight checks. I carried out this task with my usual diligence and interest. After about ten minutes, Vince walked to the aeroplane, and climbed into the right-hand seat. Aeroplanes are left-hand drive, with the captain sitting on the left, unlike our cars with the driver on the right. Vince asked me how the solo flight went. However, when I was telling him about it, I could tell from his demeanour and body language that he was not really interested, so this was not getting off to a good start. I was instructed to taxi to the hold for runway 21, where, after a short while we were given clearance to take off for circuits.

Sarcastically, Vince said, 'Let's see how you are then, now you have completed your first solo.'

Now, I am not an overly-sensitive man – at least I don't think so –

however, I did not appreciate Vince's attitude. This was not the way to encourage a student intent on becoming a PPL, paying a not-inconsiderable sum of money for the privilege of being disparaged.

On the climb out from runway 21, Vince barked at me, 'Why are you climbing out and turning here?' Questioning my turn to the right, into cross wind.

I retorted, a little sheepishly, mainly out of respect for his authority, 'Well, err, that's how Margaret taught me.'

He grunted something, and made a note on the pad on his knee board, secured to his leg. These knee boards, with note pads, are worn so that the pilot can note down instructions given by the air traffic controller (ATC) in the control tower, and can refer to them when reading back an instruction, or jot down any nuggets of information for later use. I wondered what he was writing.

We continued on the circuit, and as I turned on to the final approach, Vince again snapped at me, questioning and implicitly criticising both what I was doing and the way I was doing it. He maintained this confrontational attitude for the remainder of the lesson.

On the final circuit, I called up the tower when we were established on the downwind leg and told them the next landing would be a full stop and end of detail, and that we would be returning via the eastern taxi way to King Air.

Until this lesson, I would have done almost anything to make sure I could keep flying. However, after this experience with Vince Butler, I reflected that if I was expected to continue training with this guy as my instructor, then I would find another club, or give up.

The next day, 25th August, I returned to Biggin for another pre-booked lesson. Fortunately, and to my delight, I walked into the club and saw Margaret Butler waiting for me, with a beaming smile. She congratulated me again on how well I had flown on my first solo at Redhill Aerodrome, only three days earlier.

I was given the keys to G-BOYA and asked to start the pre-flight checks, which I did, knowing that Margaret would soon join me. This was part of the routine of every lesson, to give the student practise and ingrain the habit of checking everything out for themselves, rather than relying on the instructor. It also gave the instructor time for a cheeky cuppa.

Margaret climbed into the right-hand seat, fastened her seat belt, secured her door and said, 'OK, you carry on.'

I continued referring to my C152 check list. Once completed, with everything to my satisfaction, I started up our aerial sports car. After the usual radio exchanges with the control tower, we were soon speeding along the smooth-as-glass runway at Biggin.

Biggin Hill Airport is known by pilots, air traffic control and airline operators as EGKB. These codes are designated by the International Civil Aviation Organization (ICAO). The airport code is a unique alphanumeric code designated to each airport around the world. ICAO codes are also used to identify other aviation facilities such as weather stations, whether or not they are located at airports.

I continued to climb out of the circuit, and off into the airspace above Kent, heading towards Cliffe and Hoo.

Whilst we were in the cruise, Margaret said, 'Oh, by the way, how did you get on yesterday with Vince?'

Margaret was one of the best instructors on the airfield. I held nothing back. I relayed to her every criticism Vince had levelled at me.

Margaret responded, 'Oh dear.' She reassured me, 'I'll see him about this at home, tonight. I am very sorry, Les. I won't allow this to happen again. I'll just rearrange our lesson if something comes up.'

I would have loved to have been a fly on the wall when she arrived home that evening. Margaret was a charming woman, but did not hold back if someone needed a bollocking.

From 25th August, I started to up the ante with the frequency of my lessons. Some weeks I was having a lesson every couple of days. I completed some more solo circuits at Biggin.

On the 14th September, we started navigation training in anger. I had to plan and calculate the outward route for a flight to Lydd Airport on the Kent coast, and the return route back to Biggin. This part of the syllabus is really fun and rewarding. You draw the line of your planned route on the 1:500,000 ICAO chart, with a black chinagraph pencil. This line can be removed easily, after the flight, using your finger or a soft cloth, leaving the chart clean and ready for you to draw another line and plan another flight, another day.

In addition to my navigation training, I was simultaneously starting to learn to fly on instruments. This was only a taster, but sufficient to give a fighting chance of surviving in marginal weather conditions. I'll talk more about the instrument meteorological conditions (IMC) rating a bit later.

My planned route from Biggin to Lydd took us to the west of Headcorn airfield, onwards over Tenterden, then an approach to Lydd from the north. Lydd to a novice pilot is like trying to find a needle in a haystack, located on a piece of dead-flat land, with a few low buildings. It was quite basic in 1989 but has been developed into a much more sophisticated facility in 2021.

I called up the Lydd control tower giving the usual information – identifying ourselves, and stating our intentions. We were given permission to land on runway 23, with an instruction to report when established on the downwind leg. When you visit Lydd, the downwind leg on either runway takes you out over the sea. This is a great feeling. Flying over water, at about 800 feet, by the time you are turning on to base leg, is a novel experience. The air above the sea is unaffected by the turbulence which is typically caused by rising heat from buildings and hard terrestrial surfaces. The final approach at Lydd is also fun, coming in low over fields of cattle, grazing just a few hundred yards from the threshold of the runway.

We continued our approach and were looking straight along the concrete runway, which resembles a motorway it has so much width and length – as indeed does the runway at Biggin Hill.

After landing at Lydd, we had a detailed debrief and talked about the return route. Then, after a nice cuppa and a KitKat – a bit of sugar to keep the brain sharp – we departed Lydd, flying a reciprocal route back to Biggin.

We continued these navigation exercises flying to other, more distant airfields, including flying south to Goodwood at Chichester in Sussex. The route, via Ockham – near junction 10 of the M25 – continues overhead of Guildford, and the Hog's Back. Eventually, the white canvas-tentlike structure of Goodwood Racecourse on the top of the Sussex Downs comes into view, just north of the Goodwood Airfield, with the motor racing circuit wrapped around its perimeter.

Another navigation exercise (nav ex) destination proved more difficult to find, even for Margaret. We flew to Panshangar Aerodrome, at Welwyn Garden City; but had not intended to land there, which was just as well, because it turned out to be too elusive.

Margaret said, 'Well, we are near enough for now. We'll continue navigation training in your next lesson, so no problem. Let's head back to Biggin.'

Panshangar Aerodrome was sold to Homes England around 2017, and has been the subject of controversy since then. It was a successful general aviation aerodrome; local residents, since then, have been campaigning for the restoration of the facility 'to recreate Panshangar Aerodrome as a source of delight and pleasure for both local residents and the aviation community.'

Other nav ex destinations included Dunsfold Aerodrome and Shoreham Airport in Sussex, and Southend Airport in Essex. There were many more hours of training, until Margaret was satisfied that I was competent to navigate myself and an aeroplane around the skies of Britain.

* * *

After completing many hours of navigation training, I was on course to take my Navigation Flight Test (NFT). This was the first time that I met flight instructor and examiner, Elly Payne. I was told by Margaret to plan my route from Biggin to Lydd, which I had done and flown several times before, so this should not pose a problem. I was to fly from Biggin to the VOR beacon at Detling, then onwards to the VOR beacon at Lydd, turning at that beacon and returning to Biggin Hill.

Very-high-frequency Omni-directional Range (VOR) is a short-range radio navigation system for aircraft, enabling an aircraft with a receiving unit to determine its position and stay on course by receiving radio signals transmitted from a network of fixed ground radio beacons.

I had marked my route on my chart, which had to be kept by my side, with the magnetic compass headings written on my knee board, to refer to during the flight. It was 3rd October 1989, and the time had come for my NFT. I was introduced to Elly, who ran through what to expect during our flight.

'Have you planned the route you are going to fly?' she asked.

I answered with total confidence that I had, and was looking forward to demonstrating my flying skills and passing my NFT. I collected the keys for G BLZH, and walked out to the aircraft to carry out the pre-flight checks. Elly arrived on the apron and climbed into the right-hand seat, made herself comfortable and wrote down some notes on her knee board.

'Well, whenever you are ready, you can show me what you have learnt.' She continued, 'What is the direction and destination of our intended route?'

I told her: 'We are going to leave Biggin on the northerly runway 03, then fly to Detling VOR beacon, east of Maidstone, then onwards to Lydd VOR beacon, and return by the reciprocal route.'

I was unaware that she had taken a sneaky peek at my direction notes and headings. As usual, I taxied away from the club, to the hold for runway 03. I called up the tower, and requested permission for departure for a VFR flight to the east.

Clearance for take-off was given promptly by the control tower. I pushed the throttle fully forward, achieving full power quickly, and sped off along the smooth, grey tarmac.

Pulling back on the controls, we were soon climbing out through 400 feet. I retracted the take-off flaps. Then, I looked down at my notes, and to my horror, realised that instead of writing 'after take-off turn to the east, on a heading of 090 degrees' I had written down 'after take-off turn to the east, on a heading of 270 degrees' – exactly the opposite direction I intended to fly. I could not believe I had made such a stupid mistake, especially after Margaret's expert training, with a near-on-perfect record in every previous flight.

Resonating in my head, I could hear Margaret's warning, 'If you mess up something in the air, Elly will abandon the test, and you'll have to re-take it another time, and you will still have to pay for her time.'

I was not really concerned about the money, but the humiliation of admitting such a mistake to Margaret was not something I wanted to experience.

I just kept flying on the runway heading of 030 degrees, thinking, 'How can I cover this up?'

Now, I don't know if my error was caused by nerves at the looming prospect of this practical test, or was due to a moment of numptiness, but I realised it would be better to be honest. I looked down at my notes again. By now, we were flying at about 1000 feet so should be turning on to my heading, away from the airfield.

I confessed, 'I am afraid I've made a stupid mistake, and for some reason have put in a westerly heading of 270, instead of the easterly heading of 090.'

With a grin, and a sigh, Elly said, 'I wondered when you were going to tell me. I noticed the error when you were taxiing and thought to myself, how are we going to get to Detling by turning in the opposite direction? Circumnavigate the globe?' She continued, 'Usually, when there is a problem, and I suspect the student is not ready for the NFT, I would abort the test and return to base. However, as you've admitted your mistake, and know exactly what you've done wrong, I'm happy to continue.'

Not a good start for me, but I was encouraged by my experienced examiner's comments, and without further ado, continued to fly a perfect detail to Lydd, via Detling.

When we reached an area near Lydd, Elly said, 'I want to test you some more, to see how you would cope if you became disorientated. I have control.'

She told me to close my eyes, then she flew for a few minutes, putting the aircraft into several steep 360 degree turns.

'OK, you can open your eyes. Now, I want you to work out where we are, and navigate us a route back to Biggin.'

I looked at the direction indicator (DI) – a mechanical form of compass – and scanned the horizon for any landmark that I recognised. I began to fly on a heading of 330 degrees, and to my delight I started to recognise some landmarks; a windmill, a railway line, and immediately I knew exactly where we were. I explained how I had ascertained our location, and then described the revised, return route I would take.

We reached Biggin Hill. I landed, taxied back to King Air, and we had a cuppa, a debrief and laughed about my numpty mistake. Elly gave me the good news that I had passed my NFT. She told me that I had planned a good route, despite the directional error, had realised it as soon as I left the ground and immediately knew what to do to rectify it. This demonstrated my competence in following a route, checking it whilst in the air, and reacting promptly to a problem with concentration and confidence, rather than continuing glibly and compounding the error.

That was good to hear. 'Phew!'

This was the start of a good friendship which has lasted to the present day, even though Elly now lives in New Zealand.

Going Cross-Country

With the Navigation Flight Test behind me, the next flight test on the list is the Qualifying Flight Cross-Country (QFC). This involves a solo flight, where you leave your base airfield, navigate to another, approach and land there.

On landing, you visit the control tower, where you have to present a form to the air traffic controller on duty. They populate your form with their assessment of your radio work when first contacting the airfield and throughout the landing. They also comment on your general handling of the aircraft on approach to the airfield, including the landing and taxi to your designated parking space, and whether you shut down and leave the aircraft correctly.

Once you have had your form signed, you depart from that airfield and fly to another away-airfield, and repeat the assessment process. Finally, you depart the second away-airfield, and route directly back to your home airfield. Again, you visit the tower to collect the ATC's assessments on the form. You then hand this evidence to your instructor for inspection and comment.

Margaret and I used part of a lesson to sit down together and plan the route for my upcoming qualifying cross-country. We decided on Biggin to Goodwood Chichester, then Goodwood Chichester to Lydd, then Lydd returning back to Biggin Hill. We then followed the route on a practice flight, which was really enjoyable. I was looking forward to the prospect of flying the route solo and reaching another milestone on my route to qualification. Margaret pointed out the various landmarks along the way, including Epsom Race Course, and junction 10 of the M25, which I knew so well, having been stationary in my car at that junction so often during years of business travel in that part of the country.

Continuing south overhead Guildford, the cathedral stands out. Carrying on further south, the distinctive Goodwood Racecourse is perched on top of the Downs, near Chichester. Then, it's just a few more minutes flying time before descending on to the historic Goodwood Chichester Airfield, with its perimeter motor race track. After leaving Goodwood Airfield, a direct easterly route passes Shoreham Airport near Brighton, onwards past Beachy Head, then overhead Hastings and Rye.

Lydd is the next stop, with the nuclear power station at Dungeness as its landmark. The last leg was quite familiar, from Lydd back to Biggin Hill.

On Sunday 15th October, I drove to Biggin Hill Airport, to carry out my solo QFC. I collected the keys to a Cessna 152, G BIOM. Oscar Mike as I remember was not the best 152 on the King Air fleet, but that was the plane I was given, so out to the apron I strode, still confident in my ability to complete my QFC. I carried out the usual pre-flight checks, especially ensuring both fuel tanks, in each wing, were full to the brim. I was going to leave nothing to chance. Margaret often gave me useful tips and advice. I recalled her words, 'There is nothing more useless than a full-to-the-brim fuel bowser on the ground, when you are in the air and have run out of fuel.'

I left Biggin Hill from runway 21, and climbed out steadily to about 2000 feet, in the direction of Kenley Aerodrome. Kenley had been an important airfield during the Second World War. Now it is only used by gliders, which use a static tow line from the ground to get airborne. I gave Kenley a wide berth, as I didn't want to clash with, or impede any of the gliders that were bound to be airborne on a sunny Sunday. After Kenley, my next landmark was Epsom Downs Racecourse, with its big spectator stands, then Ockham, at junction 10 of the M25.

With the first part of my planned route ticked off my list, attached to my knee board, I turned on to a southerly heading, in the direction of Guildford. That Sunday was gloriously sunny. I was certainly in luck with the weather that day. With Guildford and its large but rather dull-looking cathedral behind me, I called up the Goodwood approach, and gave them the aircraft call sign and type, my position, intentions, and the approximate time I expected to reach the airfield. I was instructed to report when the field was in sight, and to land on runway 32.

It felt like an eternity until the buildings of Goodwood Racecourse grand stand came into view. It was quite a relief as I flew closer and could then see the entire race track below. From my vantage point, at 2000 feet above the track, I could see Goodwood Chichester Airfield. As instructed, I called up the tower requesting joining and landing instructions and reported that Golf Bravo India Oscar Mike was overhead Goodwood Racecourse.

The information I requested was transmitted immediately. I had been trained to go through the in-flight checks prior to joining the circuit and landing. I called up the tower once again, when established on the downwind leg of the circuit. I can't really recall noticing too much of the surrounding countryside whilst approaching the airfield; my concentration was focused totally on the quality of my flying. I knew that G BIOM was being scrutinised by the ATC on duty that Sunday. I do remember, on my final approach to landing, seeing lots of light aircraft parked around the airfield, and thinking to myself, 'I am almost there – one side of this triangular route complete – and on my way to becoming a qualified private pilot.'

I carried out what I felt was a very acceptable landing, and taxied to the parking area, close to the tower. Once I had given the magnetos a power check, I shut down the engine. The silence all around and my sense of satisfaction and achievement was palpable. I climbed out of Oscar Mike with a definite spring in my step. I strode confidently to the control tower, climbed the stairs, and entered the control room. The ATC on duty that day was expecting me, and had monitored my performance from first call to the airfield, until I shut the engine down at Goodwood. I was pleased to read his comments on the form, all of which were positive.

Departure from Goodwood was at 11:25. My flight would take me five miles inland of the south coast. I had the continuous way-marker of the English Channel during the flight. I flew overhead Shoreham Airport, having called up to request permission to fly overhead the field. It is not uncommon to do this, and as long as good height separation is maintained, it is quite safe to use the airfield en route as a landmark when flying cross-country.

I called up Lydd when we were in the vicinity of Hastings to request joining and landing instructions. I was given the necessary wind and runway information. The runway for this exercise was 21, so I joined the circuit on the dead side, north of the airfield, reporting once I was overhead, and then descended to circuit height, again reporting when Oscar Mike and I were established downwind.

The downwind leg of the circuit for runway 21 at Lydd is over the sea, which makes for such a smooth flight. I took a few seconds away from the intense concentration to enjoy the view across the Channel in the direction of France, and looked down at the calm sea some 1000 feet below me. All of a sudden, the end of the downwind leg had arrived. I selected twenty degrees of landing flaps and turned on to base, and was soon turning on to finals and calling the tower to tell them I was on final approach for runway 21.

The ATC replied immediately, 'Golf Oscar Mike, clear to land runway 21.' Repeating their instruction back to them, I put all my concentration into trimming the aircraft for the final descent.

Just before the runway, descending into Lydd takes you over some fields, stocked with cattle. I briefly noticed them, then was crossing the threshold of the runway demarcated with the big white number 21. I flared the aircraft, and kept the nose up whilst the lift was bleeding from the upper surface of the wings. With a little squeak from the tyres of G BIOM as it touched down, I was rolling along the concrete runway. A second landing had been completed on my qualifying flight cross-country.

Once at the exit point of the runway, the ATC gave me parking instructions. Another magneto check completed, I shut the engine down for the second time that morning and buoyantly went into the control tower to collect the signature on my form. The duty ATC at Lydd was equally positive about my flying and radio work in my approach and landing.

Having completed the formal part of my visit, I did as Margaret had suggested during the practise exercise and took some time out. With ten minutes to relax, I had a cuppa in the small café, and watched the business of the airfield from the spectator seating. My break over, I said goodbye to the staff at reception, with all the flourish of a pilot explorer. By now, I was really enjoying the day. Everything was going exactly to plan, and I was on the final leg of the QFC from Lydd back to Biggin Hill.

With clearance to take off from the ATC, G BIOM roared along the runway and climbed out into the sunny Kent sky at 12:45. My track for the return leg would take me over Tenterden, Paddock Wood, and finally overhead Sevenoaks. From there it is a short flight to join the circuit at Biggin Hill. This last part of the triangular route was quite familiar to me. Margaret and I had been flying in this part of the Kent air space during my lessons.

I was so pleased to see the familiar landmarks in this part of Kent, during my return flight. The tall church steeple at Tenterden, then the large transport distribution centre at Paddock Wood, built on a radius, which makes it easy to spot from the air. Finally, Sevenoaks, which is conspicuous by its two gasometers, and the lakes of the wildlife sanctuary. Once past those landmarks, you see the M26/M25 junction, Fort Halstead atop the North Downs, and then you are about three and a half miles, as the plane flies, from Biggin.

Once more I called up the tower to request my joining and landing instructions. I joined the circuit from the dead side, crossing over the numbers of runway 03, then turned on to the downwind leg for runway 21. At the end of the downwind part of the circuit, just as you are about to turn right on to the base leg of the circuit, another useful landmark is the British Seismological Laboratory. From above it resembles the shape of a doughnut, and by now, I could have inhaled one, let alone eaten one, or maybe two.

I reported on final approach, with confidence, having completed what felt like a mammoth journey. I landed G BIOM squarely above the numbers of runway 21, and precisely on the centre line. I presented my form to the tower, and was given the third of three entirely positive assessments.

Les Homewood had done it!

I had left Biggin Hill at 09:35, landed at Goodwood at 10:40, departed Goodwood at 11:25, and landed at Lydd at 12:25. For the final part of the test, I left Lydd at 12:45 and arrived at Biggin Hill at 13:30. I calculated I had completed two hours and fifty minutes of solo flying. A day I will never forget.

All I had to do now was to pass the aeroplane-equivalent of the driving test, the General Flight Test (GFT).

Qualification

Some days after my successful Qualifying Cross-Country Test, the day had finally come for my General Flight Test (GFT). We met in the King Air Flying Club at about 10:30. It was another sunny day, with little cloud, mainly high in the sky, so it would cause me no problems. We had a discussion, or maybe I was told what was going to happen. I was the student, and Elly had several thousand hours of flying, instructing and testing on her CV.

My aeroplane for the flight test was G BJWH, another of the Cessna 152 fleet that King Air were operating then. Whiskey Hotel was a sturdy and reliable aircraft for me to demonstrate my skills. Margaret Butler had been a fantastic flying instructor and given me the skills to attempt the GFT with confidence.

Writing in 2021, I have no idea whatever happened to Margaret Butler. During 1990 Margaret and Vince sold King Air to another flying school,

Cab Air. I believe they moved to Scotland, and I heard on the grapevine that Margaret was flying commercial freight aircraft. I would love to know where she is now, and what she has been doing for the last three decades or so.

As usual, I checked the aircraft out, then Elly joined me after about ten minutes.

'OK, Les,' she said. 'Just fly as you have been flying with Margaret, and I am sure all will be fine. I'll just sit here, and leave you to carry out the flight in the usual way. I will ask you to carry out specific manoeuvres, then you can demonstrate your capability and skill to me. OK?'

Confidently, I replied 'Yes, of course, Elly.'

I called up the tower, code switching naturally into Captain Two Voices. You might have been excused for thinking I was occupying the left-hand seat of a jumbo jet, if you heard my radio voice communicating with ATC. We departed Biggin Hill's runway 21, headed out over the Downs and followed the M25 flying east, towards Wrotham, then to the less busy air space above Cliffe, Hoo and Allhallows. There is a good chunk of Kent air space along the Thames Estuary available to use safely for instruction and tests.

Elly told me to carry out sixty-degree steep banked turns, first to the left, then the same to the right. If these very steep turns are carried out correctly and accurately, you experience running into your own wake turbulence. It's similar when a speed boat is travelling fast in a tight circle; eventually it hits its own wake in the water. I really enjoyed this part of the syllabus, sitting there with the aircraft almost vertical on its side. In a right-hand turn I was looking down towards Elly, and with a left-hand turn, I was looking directly up at her, whilst confirming how I was maintaining this attitude.

Inevitably, the GFT includes recovering an aircraft from a stall. This part of the test is repeated, simulating the aircraft experiencing problems in a range of situations: with little or no power; with landing flaps selected; at approach speed, in a bad approach to the airfield. I completed these elements of the test.

Elly said, 'Well done,' after each one, so I permitted myself a smug grin, just for a second or two.

I also had to demonstrate climbing turns and descending turns, whilst continually monitoring the aircraft. Frequently carb heat has to be applied, by pulling the control knob which forces warm air into the carburettor venturi – the tube which provides air to the carburettor. Especially at higher altitude, or on colder days, the carburettor can suffer from small ice particles forming, which then exponentially increase in size, until the venturi is totally blocked by ice. When ice blocks the air flow into the carburettor, eventually you become aware of silence, because the engine has stopped and gravity takes over.

I was constantly monitoring the fuel levels in both tanks, one in each wing. All this whilst talking on the correct frequency to air traffic control. Some limited instrument flying is included in the GFT. I have always enjoyed instrument flying; it takes intense concentration, but can be very rewarding, when you get it right, which I am glad to say I did.

After several more exercises came the worst of all – the Practise Forced Landing (PFL). This is certainly something you don't want to happen for real, but it must be mastered, just in case the unthinkable does happen. For this part of the GFT, Elly asked me to fly on a heading which took us towards Farningham – not far from my company offices. I had to react to the scenario of losing power mid-flight, first going through the procedure of checking that I hadn't turned the fuel supply off in error. Once it has been established that there is a fuel supply, the conclusion must be that the loss of power is due to mechanical failure.

I had to make a simulated mayday call to the local ATC. 'Mayday, Mayday, Mayday,' was followed by a statement of position, altitude, and number of souls on board.

The aircraft has to be trimmed to give the best angle of glide, whilst scanning the land below to choose a field that looks suitable for an emergency landing. Then, I had to brief my passenger, warning her what is about to happen, and we tightened our seat belts. The electrics in the plane had to be kept live until I was sure of reaching the field where I proposed to land. Next, after selecting landing flaps and informing ATC that the forced landing is imminent, I must turn off the master switch, loosen the latches on the doors to facilitate a quick exit, and land just as we would on any runway.

However, this was a practise forced landing, so, with about 500 feet left before we would be touching the wheels on the ground, I was instructed to apply full power, and climb away from the chosen field, back to a cruising height of around 1800 feet.

By now we had been airborne for about an hour and twenty minutes, but it felt as if I had worked an eight-hour shift, so intense is the mental concentration and physical effort involved in completing the GFT.

Elly then spoke those unforgettable words, 'Well, Les, I am pleased to say, you have passed your GFT. Congratulations.' She then asked, 'How do you want to celebrate? Would you like a barrel roll?'

Of course, delighted, I agreed with alacrity. Elly took control of Whiskey Hotel, and carried out a very smooth and controlled barrel roll. It was an amazing finish to my GFT.

We returned to Biggin, and on landing, I went back into King Air for a quick cuppa, which I felt was well deserved. However, my flying at Biggin was not quite finished for the day, as I still had another hour and ten minutes flying solo to log in order to make up the minimum total solo hours required by the syllabus.

I went back out to the apron, checked out another Cessna 152. This time I was flying in G BGOF. I proceeded to fly the necessary hour and ten minutes to secure my licence. This flight was memorable; my first solo flight after successfully completing my GFT, only fifteen minutes earlier. I departed Biggin Hill, and flew straight to East Farleigh, to circle triumphantly over our house several times.

I had such a feeling of elation and achievement. I had started my training on 11th July 1989, and successfully completed my GFT on 24th October 1989, after flying a total of forty-one hours and fifteen minutes. At that time, the minimum to qualify was forty hours.

Margaret Butler held her record at the top of the chart for getting a PPL qualified in the shortest time. All I had to do was complete this one hour and ten minutes, but I could have sat in that left-hand seat all day, soaring through the air, if I'd had enough fuel on board.

I returned to Biggin and reported to Elly that my minimum solo flying time was now completed. This final seventy minutes enabled her to sign off my GFT. The certification documents would be sent to the Civil Aviation Authority (CAA) at Gatwick, to issue my private pilot's licence. It arrived by post a few days later.

I remember driving back to the office, after a morning packed with excitement, feeling very chilled, and more than a little pleased with myself. I was unaware, whilst I was soaring elatedly above East Farleigh, that our staff and my fellow director Stan Wright were busy organising an impromptu party for me at the office.

I was told later that Mary, our company secretary, had phoned King Air to ascertain whether I had passed. They didn't want to risk organising a celebration, only for me to walk in with a grumpy face and tell them that I had failed. Once they knew that I had passed, but needed to fly off for another seventy minutes solo, it gave them enough time to get everything ready.

When I returned to West Kingsdown, expecting to get back to work, I climbed the stairs to the office, and was surprised by everyone in the office letting off party poppers. The desks were covered with tablecloths and a tempting selection of party food. Soon, champagne corks were flying in all directions. It was a truly memorable day, from start to finish, and this celebration just topped it off perfectly.

3

Private Pilot's Licence

'A satisfactory landing is one from which you can walk away.
A good landing is one after which you can immediately use
the plane again. But a total greaser is one which you
hope other pilots saw and envied.'

What Next?

After several months studying Trevor Thom flying manuals, practising and taking my flight tests, flying solo and building up my confidence, the time had finally come to take passengers. Armed with my licence received from the CAA, I was legally permitted to take passengers for a flight. And to be honest, I could not wait. After all, this is what had appealed to me, from the very start, when Stan put that crumpled piece of paper in my hand. From the very first trial lesson, I was counting down the hours, until I would be in charge of the plane as the captain. So, who was to be my first passenger?

Since Stan thought the trial lesson in a two-seat light aircraft would frighten the shit out of me, it seemed only reasonable to offer him the opportunity to experience the same. So, with this in mind, I booked a Cessna 152, G BJWH, for Saturday 18th November 1989. Stan said he would bring his video camcorder.

At this time, video camcorders were starting to be popular. They were nothing like the digital video recording equipment available now. In 1989 camcorders had only an eye-piece, which had to be held very steady, close to your eye, and the recording was made on a mini-version of the VHS tape cassette. Anyone under thirty-five who is reading this account will have to Google 'What is a VHS camcorder and how does it work?' Alternatively, ask an older person who had their heyday in the last quarter of the twentieth century.

Stan and I met at the office on the morning of 11th November and drove to Biggin Hill in my Porsche 911. Stan made a recording of some of this journey; I still have it. My 911 was one of the last to be powered by an air-cooled 3.2 litre flat-six engine, and it had a sound all of its own. It provides a marvellous backing track to the video recording of our journey. If you are a petrol-head like me, I am sure you'd agree.

When we arrived at King Air, Stan was introduced to my new friends, the instructors and Janey the receptionist and general factotum. Especially, I wanted Stan to meet Margaret Butler, whose patience and skill as an instructor had enabled me to gain my private pilot's licence.

I think I had also mastered the pilot swagger by this time, and led Stan out to the waiting aircraft, Golf Bravo Juliet Whiskey Hotel, parked on the apron on the air side of the club building. Now, I don't want to get too repetitive but, as usual, I carried out the pre-flight checks, in accordance with the Cessna 152 check list.

Soon the pair of us were rolling along the perimeter track to the hold of runway 21. During the taxiing of Whiskey Hotel, to the Alpha hold, Stan had started to take some video as a record of the flight. He adopted the customary stance of anyone using this type of equipment, with his left hand holding the camera to his eye, and his right hand operating the *RECORD* control button.

I pointed out the abundance of birds in the longer grass, either side of the taxi way; flocks of lapwings. Kentish airfields including Biggin Hill, Rochester and Lydd provide havens for these characterful, ground-nesting black and white birds with distinctive head gear. Lapwings move their wings in a slow lazy manner that creates a lapping noise, which may be why they were named lapwings. They are also called peewits, a name that imitates their display call.

Lapwing numbers have declined dramatically across Britain and this fall has been greater in southern England where farmland is increasingly used for arable crops, and pasture is improved to provide intensive grazing. *Vanellus vanellus* are now on the UK conservation Red List because lapwings need swathes of permanent, unimproved pasture-land to nest, incubate their eggs and raise their chicks. This is exactly the habitat provided by the grassy margins of airfields. Preserving local airfields also protects lapwings.

Back to our flight. After about five minutes, we were at the hold for 21 and I called the tower, 'Golf Whiskey Hotel at the hold Alpha for runway 21, ready for departure.'

In 1977 there had been a terrible accident at Tenerife Airport, when two jumbo jets collided on the runway, causing major fatalities. One of the causal factors was the mistaken belief on the part of both pilots that the clearance for take-off had been given. From that day onwards, an aeroplane will only be given the command 'cleared for take-off' after the captain has called the tower and reported in the format 'X – XXXX at the hold for runway YY ready for departure.'

So, there we were, rumbling along 21, building up speed to around fifty knots; then off we went, climbing away from the runway. Stan had the video camera to his eye, recording this, the first of many flights we would take together over the next thirty years. During the flight, out of the corner of my eye I could see Stan selectively recording parts of his first flight. I was thirty-eight and can remember thinking that it would be good to look back at this footage in years to come. It didn't cross my mind that I would still be flying when I was sixty-nine.

After flying around the skies of north Kent for about an hour, spotting landmarks and observing from an aerial perspective the county which we both knew so well, the time had come for us to return to Biggin Hill. Approaching from the east, known as the dead side, we joined the circuit for landing, calling up the control tower when Whiskey Hotel was established on the downwind leg.

I called up again on the penultimate part of the circuit, the base leg, and reported, 'Whiskey Hotel on finals to land 21.'

The reply came from the tower that Whiskey Hotel was cleared to land, runway 21. G BJWH with Stan and Les on board was now gently descending on our final approach to the runway. Landing requires intense concentration; the pilot must monitor the engine performance, the plane's speed, rate of descent and also keep a sharp look out for any conflicting aircraft in the air or on the ground.

Out of the corner of my eye, I noticed Stan raise the video camera, left hand up to his left eye, his right hand steadying it and operating the *RECORD* button. Well, that's what I thought was happening.

After landing, and just as I was steering Whiskey Hotel off the active runway, I said to Stan, 'Thanks for taking so much video, and especially the landing.'

He looked at me with an ashen face and said, 'I wasn't videoing the landing. With all of the turns during the approach and circuit, I felt sick, and when I realised that I couldn't wait until we were on the ground, I had to throw up in my camera bag!'

Inevitably, his camera bag was dumped in the first waste bin we found, as soon as we had vacated the plane. I am pleased to say that Stan is the only passenger to have been physically sick during one of my flights, from that day to this.

Flying With Family

I am not sure to this day if my wife was very keen to come flying with me for the first time. After all, driving together in a car along a metalled road is one thing, but taking off into thin air together in a small aircraft is quite another matter. Effectively, as a passenger you are entrusting your life to another person, and this can be quite daunting, the more so if the pilot is relatively inexperienced.

Anyway, Jean did agree to come flying with me. Seven days after Stan's flight, I was driving to Biggin Hill to take my wife for her first flight in a light aircraft. G BJZT was to be our steed in the sky that day. We completed the administration required to take out one of the club's aircraft, and then walked out to the plane on the apron.

Once we were both sitting in the cockpit, and with the engine running, I checked, 'Are you still OK with this, or do you want to get out?'

Jean replied, 'No, I don't want to get out; it's strange, but I'm actually looking forward to the flight.'

Without any further ado, we took off. I was at the controls of a 152, with my wife in the right-hand seat and steadily climbing away from Biggin Hill, on an easterly heading towards Borough Green. At this time, our two daughters Claire and Kate, fifteen and fourteen respectively, were regular attendees at the Crouch troop of the RHA – the Royal Horse Rangers Association.

'Shall we fly over to see the girls' riding school from the air?' I suggested

Jean agreed, 'Yes, that would be great.'

After maybe ten or fifteen minutes we were flying at 1500 feet above the ground, approaching Borough Green. Crouch is somewhat south of Borough Green, so I pushed down on the right rudder, and started a turn to my right. As I did so, a scream punctured my ears, through my headset.

I straightened up the aircraft and asked, 'Whatever's wrong?'

Jean gasped, 'What are you doing that for, making the plane go over on its side?'

Calmly, I tried to reassure her and explained, 'That's how it turns, it's not like a car, it doesn't turn horizontally, you have to put the aircraft in a banking turn.'

She made it plain she didn't want me to do that again. I responded, 'Sorry, mate, but I haven't got enough fuel on board to circumnavigate the planet and get back to Biggin without turning, so I'm afraid we are stuck with a banking turn.'

I am glad to say that, after a few minutes waiting for this information to sink in, I did manage to get the aircraft turning without her screaming in my ears. However, I had to complete the manoeuvre using only a few degrees of bank, which made the turn seem to take forever. Thankfully, after a while, she did get used to turning.

We spotted the Horse Rangers in the paddock, but couldn't be certain, from 1500 feet, which of the two riders in the group were Claire and Kate; but that didn't really matter. We knew they were there, and maybe the girls noticed a small plane circling overhead, piloted by their dad. This was a special moment; the first time I had taken a family member flying. Many more were to follow.

* * *

The next member of my family to fly alongside me was Claire, our older daughter.

To this day, Claire's younger sister Kate has never flown with me as pilot in command. Katie, by her own admission, is a very nervous flyer. If there was another way to travel to far-flung holiday destinations, she would never step foot inside a passenger jet. So, I do not take personally her refusal to join me in a Cessna, or any other aeroplane I might pilot. She always listens to my anecdotes and takes an interest in my flying.

Claire has always been the more risk-taking of the two girls; although having said that, I can recall exceptions to this statement. Both girls enjoyed riding. One Easter we took a holiday in Cornwall, staying in a lovely cottage just outside Looe, at a farm called Polpever. Here the girls rode horses across open fields, overlooking the town and the River Looe. It was idyllic.

Claire rode a very nice horse. To me, however docile the horse, it seems terrifying to be six feet off the ground, mounted on the back of an animal with a mind of its own, without any brake pedals. The horse that Kate selected was described as 'being like a Ferrari' by the riding stable owners. Kate relished having a lively mount, and galloped away with gusto, over the horizon. Ironically, Ferrari is not just an iconic sports car marque, it's one of the most common Italian surnames, and derives from the word *ferraro* meaning a blacksmith, and the root of the English word *farrier*.

During that Easter holiday, we visited Padstow, where Kate refused to join Claire and me for a power boat ride. This was no ordinary power boat; it must have been forty feet long, and took maybe six or eight passengers. Claire and I sat in the last row of seats.

The skipper took us at hyper-speed along the estuary, past the village of Rock, and out to the underwater bar where the rollers come crashing in from the Atlantic Ocean. I had to physically hold on to Claire, concerned that, with the height the boat was reaching before it crashed back down on to the waves, it could fire her over the side, like the cork out of a champagne bottle. We were both exhilarated by this experience. Returning to the quayside in Padstow, with wind-burnished faces and windswept hair to match, we found Kate and Jean sitting there, impeccably coiffed, enjoying the sun and a Cornish ice cream.

Now, to return to the main story. I drove to Biggin Hill on Saturday 20th January, 1990 with Claire. I had arranged for a friend to drive Jean and Kate to Headcorn. Claire and I would fly there to meet them all. I collected the keys to G BLZH and explained to Claire what was going on while I checked out Zulu Hotel. Looking back now, I suspect Claire might have been smiling just to humour me, rather than being enraptured by the whole procedure.

We left Biggin just after ten o'clock and made our way via Borough Green and Staplehurst to Headcorn – now known as Headcorn Lashenden. Just prior to our arrival, and during the preceding week, there had been a lot of rainfall, resulting in the grass runway, which is at almost-sea-level, being quite water-logged and boggy.

On the final approach, I could see substantial ruts in the grass runway. As soon as Zulu Hotel touched the ground, transferring its forward inertia to the grass via the three wheels, we started to snake and slide around, like a rally-cross car. Rally-cross was a popular motorsport at the time.

I am pleased to say my driving skills came in handy and I managed to prevent Z H from ending up in the adjacent field with the sheep and llamas, or in the car park on the far side of the runway. Once we had taxied to the parking area, we vacated the plane, and noticed our landing had given the underside of the wings a liberal coating of mud.

After a brief sojourn and some refreshment at Headcorn, we said our goodbyes to Jean and Kate, and departed for the return flight to Biggin. I must say, Claire took all of this in her stride, and showed no anxiety. If she felt apprehension, I was unaware of it she hid it so well.

We must have been somewhere near West Malling when I noticed another aircraft heading in our direction. The approaching plane was an American Pitts Special, an extremely manoeuvrable aerobatic biplane. I had just spotted and pointed it out to Claire, and was about to adjust our course, to keep plenty of distance between the two aircraft.

Suddenly, the pilot of the Pitts Special pulled the nose up, climbing rapidly, and carried out a partial barrel roll in the air space above us. Obviously, the pilot was experienced in aerobatics, and put neither plane at risk. Although unexpected, it was spectacular to see him upside down, performing the stunt and disappearing towards the horizon.

After another satisfactory landing at Biggin, with the added responsibility of my older daughter in the cockpit with me, I metaphorically '*ticked off*' another item from the mental list of 'things I want to achieve'. Invariably, I describe my landings as satisfactory. The majority of us PPLs are self-critical; consequently, anything short of 'a total greaser' of a landing is deemed to be 'satisfactory'.

Flying Further Afield

I continued to build my flying hours, taking a business client with me for the first time. I could only take one passenger at a time, due to the fact that the Cessna 152 is a two-seat aircraft. These dependable small planes are probably the most popular flying training aircraft in the world.

As the instructor said to me during my trial lesson, 'If you can drive a car, you can fly a plane.'

As with all aeroplane controls, if you turn the yoke or push the stick to the right, you will go right, push to the left, and you will go left, pull back towards you, and you will climb; push forward, and down you will go.

Cessnas are very stable, when travelling along during straight and level flight. You can safely let go of the controls for a moment to reach behind for your cap, to keep the sun out of your eyes, or for in-flight catering, a Mars bar and a bottle of water. The worst that will happen is a little wobble from turbulence, or you may start a slow climb or gradual descent. However, it is essential to keep checking out of the front and side windows for conflicting traffic. This may sound obvious, but if I don't mention it, someone reading this will take issue with me.

The potential to take clients flying was the main reason for learning to fly in the first place. As soon as I had my first lesson, and knew this was the hobby of choice for me, I could see the opportunities for increasing our business. Using my PPL to take a client up for a joy flight, to see their house from the air, or some other spectacular landmark would make SL stand out from our competitors. I will cover this aspect of my flying career later.

Next on my mental list of goals was to get checked out by an instructor, so that I could hire and fly four-seat aircraft. This would give me greater potential for entertaining a small group of clients, or family and friends together, rather than taking just one at a time.

I had often met Elly Payne, my GFT examiner, who later changed her name to Elly Blanche, at King Air. Our paths crossed when I was signing-in prior to taking out one of their aircraft. Or she would be there at the end of the detail, when I was filling in the technical log.

The technical log has to be completed after every flight, to keep an up-to-date record of the aeroplane's movements and report any defects that may have become apparent during the flight. Faults can then be rectified before the plane is used again by another PPL, or instructor and student.

Elly and I soon became firm friends, so it was only natural, since she was an instructor, as well as an examiner, that I would go to Elly for any further training.

On Wednesday 16th May 1990, a day after my thirty-ninth birthday, I took Stan along with me to King Air. This was not only to be the day I was being checked out to fly the four-seat Cessna 172, but we were also going to carry out a cross-Channel check. This would then enable me to take the aircraft and passengers across the twenty-two miles of the English Channel, for lunch or a day by the sea. I looked forward to spending some time in northern France, whenever other commitments permitted.

Elly ran through the preparation of a flight plan with me, which had to be completed in advance of every flight out of the UK. At that time, it had to be faxed to the Civil Aviation Authority (CAA). The plan gave details of the time we would be leaving Biggin Hill, the route we would be taking, anticipated height en route, and the time we expected to arrive at Le Touquet, our destination. The Aéroport de Le Touquet – Côte d'Opale

LFAT is about three kilometres south of the coastal town of Le Touquet in the Pas-de-Calais region of France.

This would be a momentous day, so Stan came along as guinea-pig passenger for my first cross-Channel flight. The three of us were looking forward to having lunch in Le Touquet. We had filed our flight plan with the CAA and departed Biggin at 11:35 on a lovely sunny May morning.

After climbing to our cruising height, we were soon flying over the Kent countryside, and heading towards Lydd. On approach to the coast at Lydd, we changed radio frequency to London Information – currently 124.750 MHz – and confirmed to them we were coasting out east, abeam Lydd Airport, heading across the Channel, towards Cap Gris-Nez.

Cap Gris-Nez is a chalk-cliff headland, just west of the port of Calais. This route is near enough the shortest way across the Channel that you can take. The objective is to minimise the time you are at risk of having to ditch the plane, crew and passengers in the sea, if the engine fails. Cruising at an altitude of around 3000 feet would enable the aircraft to get to the beach on either side, if the unthinkable happened and we had to glide down and make an emergency landing. On reaching the midway point between England and France, known predictably as *mid-Channel,* I changed frequency to Paris Information. The French aviation information service would already have received my faxed flight plan, and was expecting me to call them up.

I gave them the aircraft call sign, 'Golf Bravo Oscar Oscar Lima. Cessna 172. Three passengers on board. Flying at 3000 feet. Destination Lima Foxtrot Alpha Tango, Le Touquet.'

Flying over the English Channel for the first time was amazing. Seeing so many cargo vessels, of all shapes and sizes in the English Channel, called *La Manche* in France, made me understand that this narrow stretch of water really is one of the busiest, most congested straits in the world.

Vessels closer to the French coast are travelling eastwards. Those closer to the English side of the Channel are travelling westwards. It also becomes apparent when viewed from the air how many ferries are in the Strait at any time, dodging between the cargo vessels proceeding east-west along the shipping lanes. It looks like a synchronised-sailing-display on a massive scale.

Paris Information replied to my call, and gave us permission to continue our journey, tracking along the French cliffs towards Boulogne, then onwards to Le Touquet. The ICAO code for Le Touquet Calais-Dunkirk is

LFAC. We had chosen this airfield as an alternative in an emergency.

Approximately four miles from our destination, LFAT, I called up Le Touquet air traffic control, and repeated our identity information. I received airfield information, including which runway to use that day, and was asked to call them again when I had the airfield in sight.

At this point, I should remind you that Stan Wright, my business partner and best friend, was sitting in the back. Although Stan was wearing a head set, G-BOOL did not have a four-place intercom, so Stan was wearing the headset to reduce his exposure to the noise from the air-cooled engine. During the flight, if I wanted to communicate with him, I would turn around and shout, and he would lift the head set from one ear to listen to me. He could not hear the radio transmissions between me, Elly and ATC. Consequently, Stan was not aware that Elly had spoken to Le Touquet LFAT, and requested three circuits of the airfield, before landing.

Three circuits meant flying an approach to land, rolling along the runway, then applying full power and taking off again, to rejoin the circuit. And repeat. And repeat. This would give me valuable practise and familiarity with the runway at Le Touquet. Elly could then sign off my cross-Channel check. The sight of the airfield at LFAT was fantastic, close to the wide golden-sand beach. This view, combined with a scorcher of a sunny day in May and the prospect of a French lunch, made me reflect that life doesn't get any better.

Stan, unfortunately, is not an enthusiastic flyer, so when he saw the airfield, he tapped me on the shoulder, and gave me a thumbs-up, with a big smile. I smiled back, but hadn't thought to tell him we were not stopping on the first landing, or the second, or indeed the third come to that.

So, there we were, I had Oscar Lima trimmed out at a descent rate of 300 feet per minute, landing flaps of twenty degrees deployed, and air speed around seventy knots. We glided over the river, then the runway threshold and numbers, and touched the French tarmac with a respectable squeak from the tyres. I was not aware that Stan, sitting in the back, believed that, in a few minutes, the engine would stop and we would be vacating the plane. He had started to put his camera in its new bag, and had thus far avoided vomiting into it. He was preparing to get out, when I applied full power, and Oscar Lima thundered along the runway, up into the air again, to rejoin the LFAT circuit.

I called up the tower to confirm we were staying in the circuit for another touch-and-go. Again, when we had touched down on the runway, Stan prepared himself to leave the plane, surmising there had been a problem with the first landing, which had forced me to go around. By now, Stan was starting to feel ill, wanting to throw up.

You can imagine his colourful language when, after the third touch-and-go, we eventually landed on the fourth approach, stopped and he could climb out from the back of Oscar Lima. Stan had had to summon all his will power to prevent his breakfast from reappearing. He was not a happy bunny.

Elly and I were in hysterics listening to his remonstrations about the approach to Le Touquet, when he kept thinking and hoping we were about to land and stop, only for the plane to roar down the runway, taking off again, into the blue sky. All he wanted to do was to plant his feet firmly on French tarmac.

Our lunch in Le Touquet was quite brief, but nonetheless enjoyable, the more so because I had flown us there, and was going to fly us back to Biggin. We could return to Biggin Hill in little more than an hour. At 15:20 we left the lovely airfield that is Le Touquet LFAT, with its 1850 metres of smooth runway. We were soon flying over the blue-green waters of the Channel towards Biggin Hill and alighted from G – BOOL at 16:35 to go through the British Customs Check at the base of the control tower.

Not for us were the long queues at the ferry terminal. The Channel Tunnel was still under construction in 1990. It wouldn't be completed until 1991 and was officially opened on 6th May 1994. If we had chosen to travel to Le Touquet that day by car, using the ferry to cross from Dover to Calais, it would have taken a full working day. Travel to the ferry port, queuing at the ferry terminal, a ninety-minute sea crossing, passport and customs control, and then the onward drive to our destination would have taken four hours at least. And we would have had to do the same for the return journey.

Needless to say, Stan was relieved to be back on firm ground at Biggin Hill. We returned to the club house at King Air, where Elly signed my log book, recording that my cross-Channel check and type-check for the Cessna 172, had been completed satisfactorily.

As you will read later, I really did get good use out of my ability to fly the English Channel. I was becoming ever more convinced, if I needed any convincing, that my passion for flying as a private pilot would not be a short-lived flash-in-the-pan hobby. The world, or maybe more accurately Europe, was now my oyster, or better still, as Del Boy used to say in *Only Fools and Horses*, it was my lobster. Lovely jubbly.

4

More Flying Qualifications

*'You start with a bag full of luck and an empty bag of experience.
The trick is to fill the bag of experience before you empty the
bag of luck.'*

Flying in Foggles

During my initial training with Margaret Butler, and subsequent flying exams and check-outs with Elly, both of them recommended acquiring the qualification known as the IMC Rating. This stands for instrument meteorological conditions.

Let me explain about the need for an IMC. Before the 911 attack on New York's Twin Towers, which changed so much for everyone who flies, you may have had the opportunity to be invited into the cockpit of a jet airliner when travelling on holiday. I have been lucky enough to visit the flight deck on several occasions and occupy the jump seat, including on Concorde, which I'll cover later. When the aircraft is climbing away from the runway and travelling through, or cruising above cloud, you will have realised that there is no sensation of speed, or direction. Looking through a window is just like looking into a smoke-filled goldfish bowl. How does the pilot know where the plane is going and what obstacles, such as mountain ranges lie in its path?

The basic form of these conditions is known as instrument meteorological conditions or IMC. Training for the IMC rating will enable the pilot to cope much better with the job of flying the aircraft safely and reaching their destination, should they find themselves suddenly enveloped in cloud, or when a sea fog suddenly appears. One of the essentials when flying is to be able to reference the aircraft's attitude against the horizon.

Often when I flew to Le Touquet, around mid-Channel, I would tell my passengers that I was going to fly using only instruments.' This always went down well, NOT, as you can imagine. I must admit the nervous flyers were somewhat apprehensive.

I told them, 'I am now going to fly IMC, using only the instruments to fly the plane straight and level. Please keep a good look out, in case there is a break in the cloud, and inform me immediately if you see another aircraft.'

One of the benefits of the IMC rating is learning how to use the VOR beacons. Very-high-frequency omni-directional range beacons are dotted around the UK and countries across the world and are marked on CAA charts. VORs are *line of sight beacons* that emit 360-degree radio waves. With the appropriate kit installed in a light aircraft they provide a way of navigating the plane towards or away from the VOR, in any direction of the compass. VOR beacons are large, circular and easily seen from a thousand feet when flying by visual flight rules. They look a bit like a satellite dish, or maybe they are more like a huge spoked wheel, because they are flat rather than concave with a small vertical mast in the centre. They are always positioned on a plateau, with a wide clear grassy space around them, at a high point in the landscape, on the route of a flight path. They are essential for commercial aircraft navigating along international flight paths.

I had completed the statutory number of solo hours after taking my GFT to allow me to sign up for the IMC course. My obvious choice of instructor was Elly. Flying training is like any other training: learning to drive or to speak a new language, learning to drum, or to paint or prune fruit trees. If you develop trust and have chemistry with a particular teacher or instructor it's much easier to absorb the information and practise the skills being taught. If there is a choice, then the teacher whom you trust and you feel instinctively has empathy for you, whose teaching style suits your learning style, will always be the first choice. There are no barriers of distrust or dislike, and no personality clash to impede learning.

Once again, I had to purchase a Trevor Thom flight manual, and other instrument flying reference books, but this time they were all specific for the IMC rating, radio navigation, and handling of the aeroplane during adverse weather conditions.

I began my IMC training on Tuesday 10th July 1990, and since I was now qualified to fly the Cessna 172, a four-seat aircraft, G FNLY was booked out. I completed the pre-flight check.

Most of the fleet of 172s run by King Air were painted in an unusual, slightly faded, red livery. I hadn't seen any other aircraft painted like these during my comparatively short time as a private pilot. The colour wouldn't have been my first choice, if I had anything to do with deciding on the livery of aircraft. However, the colour of the paintwork does not affect the flyability of the trusty Cessna 172, or Spam Can, as some sniffy PPLs call them.

Cessna 172s are a stable and predictable platform to learn the skill of flying using instruments in what can be very challenging meteorological conditions. The disdain for the Cessna 172 arises because it is neither very difficult to fly, nor particularly energetic in the air, compared with other similarly-sized aircraft such as the Grumman American AA5b Tiger, or the French Aerospatiale Robin DR 400-180. Later, I did regularly fly both of these aircraft.

We started my training from Biggin Hill, and departed around 16:25, with a route planned to take us to Elstree Aerodrome.

During the flight, I had to navigate the aircraft whilst wearing special glasses called *foggles*. These are plain glasses but only the lowest third of each lens is transparent. The upper two-thirds are obscured, so you can't see out of the cockpit, and cannot reference the horizon or the ground, or anything else, except the instruments and your knee board and chart.

It is fundamental, and perhaps I'm stating the obvious, when flying on instruments that you use the information provided by the instruments on the flight panel – the equivalent of the dash board in a car – to maintain straight and level flight. This skill is achieved by constantly scanning the instruments but paying particular attention to the artificial horizon (AI). This key instrument shows a circle split in two. The upper half, above the diameter line, is blue, representing the sky, and the lower half, is black, which represents the ground. As you bank the aircraft to the left, it will show the right hand, or starboard wing, rising into the blue upper half, and the left or port wing descending into the black lower half. Oppositely, as you bank the aircraft to the right, it will show the left, or port wing, rising into the blue upper half and the right or starboard wing descending into the black lower half.

The vertical speed indicator (VSI) is an instrument which indicates the rate of climb or descent of the aircraft. The VSI calibrates and shows in feet per minute whether you are descending or ascending, confirming your aircraft's attitude.

In addition to these instruments, you have an air speed indicator (ASI), which performs the same task as the speedometer in a car. The ASI will let you know if your air speed is decreasing. When the nose is raised and the aircraft is ascending, speed decreases and this can induce a stall, resulting in a total loss of lift, with potentially disastrous consequences. If the plane is descending, nose down, the ASI will show a rapid increase in airspeed. This can over-rev the engine, may cause mechanical damage, and if not checked, inevitably results in controlled flight into the ground.

The heading indicator (HI), marked with the four cardinal points of the compass and the degrees between them, is also referred to as the direction indicator (DI). This instrument is used to inform the pilot of the aircraft's heading or bearing.

We navigated our way to Elstree, and landed. Once we were on the ground, we had a de-brief, a quick drink – tea, of course – and flew the return route to Biggin Hill, during which I continued to practise flying on instruments.

IMC training covers the elements of flying a plane when there is limited visibility due to adverse weather conditions. Navigation cross-country, between the VOR beacons I have already mentioned. Another key skill is to learn to fly an instrument landing system (ILS) approach. This is perhaps the most highly-charged and challenging flying a PPL can do. The ILS approach is used by jet airliners when flying into the world's airports. Intrinsic to the ILS is the marker beacon, a particular type of VHF radio beacon, used in conjunction with ILS receivers installed in the aircraft to give pilots a means to determine the position of their aircraft along an established route to the destination runway.

The marker beacons are located at specific distances. At Biggin Hill there is an outer beacon and an inner beacon. When flying the ILS approach, you must watch the instrument on the flight panel, which has two perpendicular needles. One of them will travel from left-to-right then right-to-left, the other one will travel from top to bottom and bottom to top. When the needles cross each other at the dead centre of the instrument, you know you have the aircraft on the right track towards the runway. You are on the correct glide slope on the final approach to the runway. This, I would say, is the hardest part of the IMC rating, and it took much practise to get to the stage where I was capable of landing an aircraft this way, and safely.

During the intense IMC training, another task was to carry out precision approach by radar (PAR). This was satisfying to complete and gave me an amazing endorphin rush.

By now, I was getting proficient at flying whilst wearing the foggles, so Elly used to make me wear them on the climb out, after five hundred feet. This never concerned me; I knew she was keeping a look out to see if any other aircraft were dangerously close to us. I was enjoying my new skill of flying the aeroplane referring only to the instruments.

After leaving Biggin on 19th July, we made haste, in the direction of the Ockham VOR beacon to the west of Biggin Hill, close to junction 10 of the M25. From there, Elly called up Farnborough ATC, and requested a PAR approach.

Farnborough ATC then spoke directly to me, giving me radar directions known as vectors. We were approximately six miles from Farnborough when the exercise started. We were simulating a situation in which a sudden fog had closed in, and I could not safely reach another airport using the

VOR/ILS approach system. So, I would have to call up an appropriately equipped airfield, such as Farnborough.

I was given headings to fly and told the height I had to maintain. As we flew closer to Farnborough, the instructions became increasingly precise. Elly explained that the radar equipment they had at Farnborough was so accurate they could see the aircraft as a 3D image, including air speed and rate of descent.

The tension was palpable, but I was enjoying the challenge. Initially, ATC was giving me headings which were maybe ten degrees off the heading I was on. I repeated each instruction and followed it. We were getting ever closer to Farnborough.

The advice came from a reassuringly calm voice, 'You do not have to repeat my instructions.'

The ATC then told me, 'Reduce speed to seventy-five knots, turn one degree to the left.' To achieve this required only a kick on the left rudder from me.

Confirmation came from Farnborough, 'You are on the correct glide slope and path.' The sequence of instructions continued for what seemed an age, but was probably only four or five minutes.

Still, I could not see out of the windows because of the foggles. Elly told me that we were on a very short final approach to the runway at Farnborough.

'Les, we are on short finals, do you want to look up now, or continue a bit longer?'

I replied, 'No, let's go on, this is amazing.' I continued listening to and complying with the instructions given by ATC.

Then Elly said, 'OK, that's it, you can look up now.'

I removed the foggles, and to my delight and complete astonishment, Elly, Lima Yankee and I were about thirty feet above the runway threshold number 24 at Farnborough.

Elly called ATC, thanked them for their help, and said we would now fly the runway, climb out and return to Biggin Hill.

This happened *thirty* years ago, but it still gives me such a buzz when I recall the experience. It is reassuring to know that here, in the UK, if ever I were to get into real difficulty with fog right down to the ground, there is this professional service available to private pilots, to keep us, our passengers and the plane safe.

After experiencing the amazing IMC Precision Approach Radar flying into Farnborough, I still had some more hours of practise to complete. These we carried out at Lydd Airport.

On Thursday 23rd August, at around 14:40, we departed Biggin Hill in a Cessna 172, call sign G-BOOL. Oscar Lima, you may recall, was the 172 I flew for my cross-Channel check-out. We had already contacted Lydd ATC and explained our intentions, so when we arrived, I flew several ILS approaches wearing the dreaded foggles. I practised holding patterns prior to joining for a procedural approach and landing.

Let me explain. A 'holding pattern' is the name for the procedure you may have experienced when you are returning from a trip abroad.

The captain says, 'There will be a slight delay before we can land. We have been asked to remain in a holding pattern. We apologise for the delay.'

This means the aircraft cannot land due to either an obstruction on the runway, or more commonly, too many aircraft trying to land. So, you fly over a VOR beacon near enough to the airfield, using it as a marker. From there you fly in a straight line for a distance, then make a one-hundred-and-eighty-degree turn, and fly back in a straight line, in the opposite direction, at exactly the same height, back to the VOR beacon. This is the race-track pattern. When you get to the end of that straight line, you carry out another one-hundred-and-eighty-degree turn, and so on. You continue to do this until ATC calls you, and gives you permission to descend, and continue your approach to land at your destination airport.

Anyway, back to G-BOOL. I had to complete several tasks that day, including radar-vectored ILS approaches. When I was some three miles from Lydd Airport, the ATC would give me radar vectors or headings to fly towards the airfield. There I would intercept and pick up the ILS approach signal and fly towards the designated runway.

An essential skill to master is recovery from different attitudes in cloud. Believe me, recovery from a stall with clear sight of the ground and the horizon is one thing, but if the aeroplane gets into a stall, or spiral dive in IMC conditions, it is quite another matter.

Stall recovery when flying visual flight rules (VFR) is not too difficult. Well, I didn't think so, after the initial shock that first time and when I had done it a few times. When you have visual reference to the horizon, and the ground below, you can utilise all of your senses.

However, if you are unfortunate enough to allow the aircraft to develop a stall, or get into a spiral dive when in cloud, you have neither the horizon, nor the topography of the ground beneath you as reference points. It will serve absolutely no purpose to look out of the window. To add to the dilemma is the fact that your physiology is working against you, when your plane is in a spiral dive or descent.

Your head has some plumbing, just inside your ears, called the eustachian tubes. These are small passageways that connect your throat and the back of your nasal cavity to your middle ears, one each side. When you sneeze, swallow or yawn, your eustachian tubes open; this keeps air pressure and fluid from building up inside your ear. Your ears pop when pressure in the ears needs to equalise, so that your eardrum doesn't expand or contract more than usual and suffer barotrauma. In certain environments, such as when travelling in a lift in a skyscraper, when scuba diving or when taking off or landing in a jumbo jet, you can become uncomfortably aware of your eustachian tubes.

When you are sitting in a small aeroplane, obviously you aren't connected to the ground, consequently you have no direct connection with gravity. Your inner ears control your perception of forward and backward motion, and the sensations of rising, falling and turning. Your inner ear can be confused about your direction of travel, and cannot relay this information correctly to your brain. If you were travelling in a car, and you kept going around and around counter-clockwise, turning to the left, your right ear would detect the motion, telling your brain you are turning left.

Imagine then, that you are sitting in the cockpit of a light aircraft, in a spiral dive, descending at more than five hundred feet per minute, and you can't see anything out of the window. After a couple of rotations, your ears are popping and your brain decides to ignore the confusing messages from your sensory organs, your ears and your eyes. Neither of these sensory organs have evolved to cope in this unnatural situation. This is instrument meteorological conditions where your instruments are your only salvation.

By scanning the vertical speed indicator, you can tell whether you are going up or down, or travelling straight and level. You must scan both the magnetic compass and direction indicator, which will be spinning one way or another, telling you that you're not going in a straight line. You will also be scanning your air speed indicator, which will either be increasing rapidly if you are descending, or will be decreasing rapidly if you are climbing too much, heading into a stall. Only by correlating the information from the instruments, will you be able to decide which directional and power inputs are needed. Adjusting the ailerons, rudder, elevator and engine will enable you to recover control of the aircraft.

I hope all of that makes sense. In short, in IMC conditions, you must have total faith in what your instruments are telling you. You must not think that they might be wrong. You will have checked all the instruments are working prior to take off. Only by developing skill in reading the instruments, and responding to what they tell you, will you be safe in IMC conditions.

We left Lydd later that day, after some very intense flying training, looking forward to the IMC test. I am pleased to record; I took the IMC test the next day on 24th August 1990. It lasted a little over two hours and I passed the test well, flying to a good standard. At least that is what's written in my log book. I had another qualification under my belt, which would later save my life when unintentionally tested in a real emergency situation.

Now for a Big Boy's Toy!

Through the rest of 1990 and during 1991 I kept up quite a busy flying schedule. I had now progressed to flying Piper low-wing aircraft. These feel totally different in the air when compared with the Cessna 172. The Cessna is a safe and predictable aeroplane to fly; does that mean it should be distained as a Spam Can? I think not, but it was a natural progression to develop my flying skills on other types of aircraft.

I used to fly a Piper Cadet, with the appropriate call sign of G KDET. This was the first aeroplane in which my parents would fly with me. I have a wonderful photo of my mum and dad standing next to G KDET. To be honest, I think Dad was quite nervous, but my mum had total faith in my ability as a pilot. Even at the age of forty, it felt the same as when I'd just swum my first width at the local swimming baths; she was so proud of me.

We took off from Biggin Hill, and I flew them over south-east London and into Kent, over the places they knew so well on the ground. Throughout the flight, my mum never stopped talking and pointing out the landmarks that she recognised beneath us. My dad, on the other hand, was noticeably quiet. I am sure he was not comfortable about being in the skies above Kent, with me at the controls. He was a very nervous passenger in a car, although he enjoyed driving all his life. He might have found the whole experience terrifying, but he controlled his nerves enough to get into the plane to fly with Mum. They did everything together and I admire him for overcoming his anxiety in order to be with Mum, and let her really enjoy the experience. After a good flight, I returned them safely to Biggin Hill.

On the day that I first took my parents for a flight, I had taxied past a twin-engine aircraft, standing taller and looking like a real handful. I thought, 'Now that is something I would like to fly.' A mental note was taken and obviously the next step was to contact Elly, and enquire about obtaining a twin rating, and ask her what was involved.

'No problem,' was Elly's reply. 'You'll pick it up easily.'

So, I arranged for my first lesson in a twin-engine plane on Wednesday 9th October 1991. I would be learning how to fly a multi-engine aircraft using a Grumman American GA7 Cougar. As twin-engine aircraft go, the GA7 is not the most powerful, but it is a dependable aeroplane to learn on, and it takes as much skill to master as any other twin.

We started ambitiously and filed a flight plan for Le Touquet. Elly had suggested that the longer cross-Channel journey from Biggin to Le Touquet would give us plenty of time to go through the usual flying exercises and for me to learn how to handle the complexities of a bigger, twin-engine plane. Effectively, all the flying exercises that apply in a single-engine aircraft apply to a twin, but on a considerably larger scale. To begin with, when carrying out the pre-flight checks, there are two engines to check, and two propellers to monitor for chipped blade edges or cracks.

When the engines start up, it does feel like stepping up to a whole new league of flying. Once the port engine is running nicely, and the procedure is repeated for the starboard engine, the resulting noise and vibration combined with anticipation of the flight definitely triggers the production of dopamine, the happy hormone. As it coursed through my blood stream, it seemed to affect my facial muscles. I just couldn't stop smiling as I looked at those two propellers spinning around in the idle rev range, ready to fly.

After taxiing to the hold, we were given clearance to line up. Now, at the threshold of the runway just before take-off, instead of just one lever to push forward for the throttle I had four levers, and this makes the twin-engine aircraft a real big boy's toy. Sitting in the left-hand seat of the GA7 Cougar, with four levers to operate, is so different from flying the Cessna 172 or any other single-engine aircraft. The GA7 has two throttle levers, one for each engine, and two levers for the propellers.

The GA7 is fitted with variable pitch propellers. A variable pitch propeller is one in which the pilot is able to adjust the blade pitch during flight. The blade angle can be adjusted to its optimum value for the phase of flight – during take-off, climb or cruise. The propellors are controlled by means of a constant speed unit (CSU).

For take-off the propellers are configured coarse, with the two blue-topped levers fully forward, which gives maximum lift but makes a lot of noise, and is not so efficient in the cruise. Therefore, when you are climbing away from the runway, after about 500 feet, you pull the two throttle levers back first, followed by the two propeller levers, so the propellers are working to a finer pitch, (2300 rpm on the throttle, and 2300 rpm on the propellers). The plane will now travel faster and quieter, with further adjustments to both during the cruise.

The CSU also enables a propeller to be feathered or to free wheel if the engine becomes inoperable, allowing the propeller on the dead engine to windmill in the air stream, reducing its drag effect, whilst the good, still functioning engine and propeller continue to fly the plane. I could ramble on for pages on the minutiae of the controls, but I won't.

With the propeller levers fully forward or coarse, I pushed the throttles to 2000 rpm and checked all the flying instruments, the oil temperature and pressure. When I was happy that everything was working well, I pushed the throttles the rest of the way to the stops, giving us full power. We picked up speed at a surprising rate. This really was something I'd never forget. We lifted from the runway at Biggin at around eighty knots indicated air speed, I retracted the undercarriage, for the first time, and continued heading south.

Both Elly and I flew G PLAS high above Kent that morning, in the direction of Lydd and the Kent coast. We were travelling at around 4000 feet by the time we reached the coast and headed out over the English Channel. We called up the usual FIR contacts – Paris first, then Le Touquet on approach. We asked for some circuits on arrival, so that I could practise landing and take-off in the GA7, and simulate an emergency. Losing an engine on take-off can happen, although fortunately not very often. It is therefore essential to know how to cope in that circumstance. As a point of interest, circuits were cheaper at Le Touquet than at Biggin Hill in 1991.

Together with the extra levers for throttles and propellers, and extra gauges to monitor, there is the added delight of having a retractable undercarriage. A significant milestone for a PPL who is working his way up the aviation scale is to start flying a plane with wheels that retract on take-off. The Cessna and Piper Cadet both have fixed undercarriages.

When flying the GA7 it is important not to forget to put the wheels down when returning to land. To this end, when flying an aircraft with a retractable undercarriage, on the final approach to any airfield ATC permission to land includes a question.

'Do you have three greens?'

This refers to the green lights, one for each wheel, that illuminate on the dash when you lower the wheels; they go out when you retract the wheels.

So, when the tower asks for the confirmation, your reply is, 'Cleared to land with three greens.'

Then everyone knows you haven't forgotten something vital, and you will avoid an awful, noisy scraping sound when skidding along the runway on the fuselage, to be followed by a very expensive repair bill.

Some of the in-flight emergencies you train for are quite physical to master. In the unlikely event of an engine failing in a twin-engine plane, the upside of that predicament is that you still have an engine making lots of noise and doing its best. Depending on the horsepower of the engine and weight of the aircraft, flight continues. Whereas, in the case of engine failure in a single-engine plane, gravity takes control of the situation and descent is inevitable.

With any upside, there is always a downside. The downside is that the engine which is still working is now trying to push the plane to the side where all has gone quiet. This results in quite a violent veer to the side of the failed engine and requires a hefty boot full of rudder to maintain straight flight asymmetrically.

There is a mnemonic that you are taught '*dead leg, dead engine*'. When Elly put me to the test, it was always unannounced. She would be talking to me, wait until I was looking the other way out of the window, then she would quietly and slowly move her hand to the engine fuel supply valves, turning off the fuel to one engine.

Immediately, if she cut the port side engine, on the left, the plane would lurch to the left, which required a very strong push down with the right leg on to the right rudder pedal. The other leg, the left leg, would be doing nothing, as all my strength was used to keep the plane straight using my right leg. The left leg was effectively a dead leg, not working, just like the left engine.

This procedure identified the failed engine before you even looked out of the window. The GA7 has a rudder trim, as well as an elevator trim, so I would quickly trim the rudder, putting more bias to the right-hand side, which alleviated the force I had to exert on the rudder pedal with my right leg. This procedure was to maintain the aircraft in level flight, whilst investigating the cause of the engine failure. Maybe the fuel had been turned off by mistake, or maybe there was an engine fire.

If the engine could not be re-started, an emergency pan-pan-pan call, rather than a mayday call, is made because the aircraft is not in immediate danger. The pan call is made on the ATC frequency to which your radio is currently tuned to inform them of the situation, requesting an immediate approach and landing at the nearest airfield.

Once you are established in the circuit to land at the nearest airfield, after a Pan call, everything is carried out as for a normal landing. All the pre-flight checks are carried out in the usual manner. The only difference with this simulation, or if the situation were for real, is on the final approach. With the wheels down on finals, landing flaps are not deployed until you are sure you can reach the airfield, and that the runway is free from any obstacles. This is precautionary. For instance, should the landing flaps be deployed too early in the final stage of approach, then at three hundred feet above runway level, you notice an obstruction on the runway which makes it unsafe to land, it would be necessary to abort the landing and go-around. Not all twins, and I include the GA7 in this, would have the grunt on one engine to successfully climb away from the runway to attempt a second landing. So, the flaps are left until you are totally certain that you can make the runway, and there are no obstructions to impede safe landing.

We did put this to the test once at Rochester Airfield. We had an engine throttled back, giving no lift, but still there ready. We made an approach and went for a go-around at about two hundred feet, simulating a runway obstruction at the last minute. We adjusted the flaps from landing mode to the take-off configuration, and pushed the throttle to give the one working engine full power. To our astonishment and delight, G PLAS slowly but surely, started to climb. The best it managed, I recall, was around a hundred feet per minute. This was not ideal but better than nothing, and would have given a reasonable chance of making another approach for a safe landing.

We continued my training on the return flight from Le Touquet to Biggin, landing back in Kent at around half past two. I had been flying for three and a half hours that day. Since I was determined to gain the qualification, we repeated the cross-Channel journey, and I completed more training exercises the next day, 23rd October.

Le Touquet was a popular choice for training in those days. As well as being less expensive than Biggin Hill for circuits, it was also relatively quiet, so there was not too much pressure put on the pilot in the circuit.

My twin rating flight test examiner was a man called Cyril Knight. Cyril was a mature aviator with a warm, friendly personality. I met him at Biggin. We were flying in G PLAS. I remember that, on the day of the test, he had a streaming cold. As he buckled his harness, seated next to me, he apologised for sneezing and coughing. This didn't worry me at all; I had too many other things on my mind. I wanted to pass my twin rating first time. I didn't want to spoil my record of achievement and let down my instructor, or myself. More than that, I wanted to fly this big boy's toy and share the joy with family and friends. Suffice it to say, Cyril was suitably impressed with my handling of the GA7. I had satisfactorily completed all the elements of the test.

Cyril announced: 'Les, I am pleased to say you have passed your twin rating.'

I believe Cyril had been in the RAF at some time, because whilst we were returning to Biggin Hill, Cyril noticed, in the distance, an old Auster aircraft, painted in military colours and markings. We had heard the pilot in radio communication with Biggin ATC telling them where he was operating, explaining that he was staying at low level, about 500 feet, taking aerial photographs of houses.

A brief aside. The Auster was produced by Taylorcraft Aeroplanes (England) in Leicestershire, during the Second World War. The name was borrowed from Roman mythology in which Auster was the spirit of the sirocco wind, blowing from the south, which brought heavy cloud cover and fog or humidity. Some 1600 of these high wing monoplanes were built. Classified as light aircraft, they were used for British military liaison and aerial observation during the war. Briefly post-war they were used for counter-insurgency and casualty evacuation, until military helicopters took over that role. So, to see this Auster being flown to do a job of work in the early nineties was a bit of a rarity. But what happened next was a real treat.

Suddenly, Cyril said: 'I have control, Les.'

He put G PLAS into a steep spiral dive, descending at great speed towards the Auster, then at a respectable height above it, Cyril levelled off Alpha Sierra.

With a huge ear-to-ear grin, he said, 'We could have shot him out of the sky, and he wouldn't have known what had hit him!'

He returned control to me and said, 'Les, you have control. Let's get back to Biggin, and have a cuppa. Well done, Les, good flying.'

Cyril signed my log book, and I had another qualification to my name. Yours truly was still enjoying flying, gaining experience and learning new skills. I mused. 'What next?'

Should I Eat More Carrots?

Next came my night rating. Before I begin in earnest, describing the different places I have flown to, the aircraft that I have flow, and telling you tales of the unexpected, the amusing, the bizarre and quite scary incidents that have punctuated my flying life, I will tell you about my training for the night rating.

There's an old joke.

Pilot:	Will eating more carrots help me to see in the dark?'
Greengrocer:	Well, you never see a rabbit wearing glasses, or a head torch. They see well enough in the dark. How many would you like?

We now jump forward to 1994. To be precise, 9th December 1994, for that is the day, or should I say night, that I started training for the night rating. I can't really recall what prompted me to take this rating. However, when you think about the prospect of being airborne in the pitch black, looking down at the city, suburbs, towns and villages, all lit up like Christmas scenes, why wouldn't you want to? Unless, of course you are terrified of flying, which would be a good reason to choose a different hobby like knitting, golf or crown green bowls.

I retrieved my training manuals from the loft and spent plenty of time boning up on the chapters covering the dos and don'ts of flying after sunset – the night rating.

One of the subjects covered in the manual is 'aircraft icing', since the night rating would be of more use in the winter than the summer. This icing has nothing to do with creating dainty swirls of frosting with a piping bag. I am talking about the hard, white stuff, or the even more deadly transparent ice that can build up on an aeroplane's wings, elevator, ailerons and any other surface or moving part.

Sadly, there have been too many aircraft disasters caused by ice build-up on aircraft wings and other surfaces. So, this subject is not one to be taken lightly. On a few occasions, Elly and I left the clubhouse of Surrey and Kent Flying School at Biggin Hill, and had to de-ice the upper surface of the wings prior to flying, using a proprietary de-icing solution. Although the ice was a mere film, this could soon develop into a more substantial layer, and degrade the lift from the upper surface of the wings, leading to disaster.

After de-icing, and carrying out the usual pre-flight checks, we taxied away from the apron on the air side of Surrey and Kent Flying School at about 17:30. It was dark, so we followed the small piercing blue lights that lead you to the runway.

Inside the plane, which was Elly's own Cessna 152, call sign G BJZT, the instruments lit with a red glow. Red light is used on the instruments and torches used inside the aircraft to allow the pilot to read the instruments and maps, whilst also visually scanning the environs of the plane. Red light enables scotopic vision, or dark-adapted eyes, in low light conditions – objects are visible but appear in black and white.

It is an entirely novel sensation, taxiing to the hold of the runaway at night. There is very little to reference in the environs of the aircraft in the dark. Airfields are laid out so that there are no buildings or obstructions for the wings to collide with near the runway. Any potential obstructions, like the buildings on the airfield, are lit up at night. All you can see outside is blackness, apart from those piercing little blue taxi way designation lights, which lead you to the holding point.

You cross the double white lines, on to the active runway, only after ATC have given permission. Once at the hold, we were given the departure information we had to adhere to once airborne, and were given the radio frequency for Thames Radar FIR, with which we would communicate during our local training flight.

Taking off in the dark, for the first time, is a very strange experience. You are immediately immersed in something akin to sensory deprivation. For the first hundred feet or so you have the nose of the plane in an upward position, and there is nothing to refer to; no buildings or horizon are visible so the initial climb out is on instruments.

Once you are established in the climb and gaining height, street lighting and illuminated buildings, or the glow of a distant town on the horizon, give you some visual reference. Then it begins to feel more normal. After departure from Biggin Hill's runway 21, we headed south to intercept the M25.

With all of our navigation lights flashing, we resembled a Christmas tree. Red on the left or port side, and green on the right or starboard side, combined with the landing light. Landing lights are usually set into the leading edge of the wings or sometimes into the front of the nacelle, which is equivalent to the bonnet of a car. All this illumination helped our conspicuity, making Zulu Tango visible to other aircraft that were sharing the same air space.

The first time I flew Zulu Tango in the dark was quite magical. We were soon flying over the M25, and below us there were two amazing lines of bright red vehicle rear lights, streaming along on their homeward journey. On the opposite carriageway, there was a constant stream of bright white vehicle head lights. They looked like the lights on a giant pinball machine. Elly allowed me a few minutes to admire this incredible sight, which few people have the pleasure of witnessing.

When night flying, the CAA 1:500,000 chart is even more essential as a tool for navigation than when flying in daylight. What you are able to see from the air, in the dark, is extremely limited. On the charts, the significant villages, towns, and cities are highlighted in yellow, corresponding to the overall shape of the settlement, when seen from above.

I was told that the shape on the chart closely replicates what you see from the air. When the shape of a town on the chart resembles a yellow horizontal diamond-shape, then the lighting from that town will be recognisable as a horizontal diamond-shaped glow in the landscape.

Chart reading and radio communication with London Information and Thames Radar provided me with sufficient information by which to navigate. I also had Elly Blanche in the aeroplane with me, whom I trusted totally to train me to become a confident night flyer. Using our prepared route, we headed south towards Tenterden.

Based on the estimated timing on our flight plan, when I thought we should be overhead Tenterden I looked down. It was a revelation. I could identify the town of Tenterden because its glowing shape corresponded exactly with the shape on the chart.

From Tenterden, our next waypoint on the plan was Sittingbourne. We flew over Ashford and out towards the Downs. However, the Downs were not visible in the dark. Our flight to Sittingbourne was another opportunity to take in the shapes of the brightly-lit towns and villages beneath us, and notice that even small hamlets and isolated houses are visible from the air.

I reflected on the critical importance of blackout regulations during the Second World War. I now understood why blackout regulations were strictly imposed across Britain on 1st September 1939, the day Hitler invaded Poland and before the official declaration of war. Blackout regulations required that all windows and doors should be covered at night with heavy curtains, cardboard or paint, to prevent the escape of any glimmer of light that might assist enemy aircraft with their navigation. The regulations also affected travel on the roads after dark; street lights were unlit throughout the war, and bicycle and vehicle lights had to be dimmed. There were posters to show people how to do this.

From Sittingbourne, we changed our heading to a westerly direction, then called up Thames Radar to communicate our intention to return to Biggin Hill. They handed us over to Biggin approach when we were about three miles from the field.

I called up Biggin approach, gave them our full call sign to request joining and landing instructions. A prompt response from the tower provided me with the QFE. With this information, which relates to the setting of the altimeter, we joined the circuit for what was to be my first landing in the dark.

As usual, our approach to the airfield was overhead, at the far end of the runway where any aircraft would be below us, on their take-off run. I looked down on to the apron in front of the control tower at Biggin. I could see a couple of business jets parked and illuminated on the ground by localised lighting. This just added to the whole phenomenal experience.

Once I had established our track on the downwind leg of the circuit for runway 21, I looked over my right shoulder to the runway, but could not see it at all. The runway lights are only visible from the approach path. When you think about it, if you could see the runway lights from any angle it would be disastrous, with aircraft approaching to land from several directions.

I turned from downwind on to the base leg, then shortly on to finals. I called up the tower again.

In my best Captain Two Voices accent, I announced, 'Golf Zulu Tango, on finals to land runway 21.' The tower replied, giving me permission to land and wind direction.

That final approach was just incredible. I really can't think of a word that sufficiently describes the experience. Seeing that huge runway, with super-bright lights showing me the safe track to the ground, and the Precision Approach Path Indicators (PAPI).

When you are established on the correct glide slope, you will see four lights, TWO red and TWO white.

If you see FOUR white lights you are too high. When you see FOUR red lights, you are too low.

It was the perfect finish to my first foray into night flying. I had Zulu Tango trimmed for a 300 feet per minute descent. The speed was perfect, and suddenly there we were, gliding over the piano keys – the black and white alternate stripes above the runway designation numbers on the tarmac. I held the nose of the aircraft up and the two main wheels gently made contact with the runway, the nose wheel doing the same a moment later. The tower called up and gave the instruction to taxi to the end of the runway, then depart. Once off the active runway, we followed those beautiful, piercing bright blue lights back to the apron outside Surrey and Kent Flying School. I had done it. I had flown at night for the very first time.

During my next night rating lessons, I had to complete lots of solo circuits, so I could get used to the feel of flying in the circuit in the dark, as well as the sensation of the take-off and the approach in the dark. Also, I had to practise local navigation and liaison with Thames Radar for navigation assistance.

Some landing approaches back to Biggin were made with a request to the tower to switch off the PAPIs so I could gain the skill I needed to keep my glide path correct for landing, by using my own judgement with only the runway lighting.

On one occasion, when we were on our final approach to runway 21, the lights were really bright. Like cars that hadn't dipped their headlights.

Elly said to me, 'They're bright, too bright.'

She called up the tower and asked for the lights to be turned down a bit. To my surprise, they agreed. Instantly the lumen level of the lights gradually reduced, just like turning the dimmer switch in the living room at home.

I took my night rating flight test on 20th January 1995. Fortunately for me, the weather was kind, with no severe icing problems, and no rain. I passed this flying test at the first attempt. Captain Two Voices now had 'Night Rating' to add to the other qualifications recorded in his log book.

Aerobatics

After successfully completing my night rating course, I was at Biggin Hill one day, and encountered Elly as she returned to Surrey and Kent Flying Club.

We had a cup of tea and catch-up. As usual, we started talking about the joys of aviation. Elly said she was teaching a student to fly aerobatics. I asked her about aerobatic flying. Enthusiastically, she described in some detail the flying techniques and exercises for the aerobatic qualification. It really appealed to me. Other than experiencing the barrel roll that Elly flew at the end of my GFT, I had never flown any aerobatic manoeuvres. I had seen plenty of aerobatic displays by the Red Arrows, and other aircraft and helicopters at various air shows over the years.

I am sure you're ahead of me already.

'That sounds great fun. When can we start?' I asked.

My justifying thought was that mastering some aerobatic manoeuvres would give me more confidence in the air, which can only be a good thing for any pilot. However, my real motivation was the prospect of flying an aircraft through a 360-degree loop, and seeing the ground where the sky should be. And that's an awesome prospect.

I had two or three aerobatic lessons with Elly. On one occasion we flew to Le Touquet as part of my IMC renewal test. The longer journey between EKGB and LFAT gave us plenty of time to practise some aerobatic manoeuvres. We also used Kent air space for my training lessons.

Without referring to my log book, I can still remember the sequence of flying a loop in G BJZT. After we had checked our height, and the air space around us, to ensure that it was safe to start the manoeuvre, it went thus:

Set power to 2200 rpm, establish the aircraft in a shallow dive, and when you reach 120 knots indicated air speed, pull back on the controls, keeping the rudder central.

Then, as the nose of the aircraft climbs through the horizon, apply full power, maintaining back pressure on the controls all the time.

Look up through the plexiglass panels in the roof, and you will see green fields where normally there would be sky. Still keeping back pressure on the controls, on the downward part of the loop you are briefly looking straight through the windscreen at the ground rushing up to greet you.

As you get to the bottom of the loop, returning to straight and level attitude, ease the throttle back to your cruise power of around 2100 rpm.

Oh yes, then you can start to breathe again!

I mention this because during your first attempt at flying a loop, you are concentrating so intently that breathing seems to be a distraction from the thrill of flying upside down.

On the second loop I flew, the initial nerves and apprehension did go and I was able to breathe. Then it's possible to really appreciate the sensation of increasing speed in the dive. Another fantastic moment is pulling straight up from that dive and feeling your body being pushed into the seat by the g-force, caused by the change in the aircraft's attitude, when you go into a sudden climb. As your gaze switches from the screen to the panels in the roof, the view of the ground that you get whilst your neck is stretched, monitoring the manoeuvre is incredible. I cannot overstate the feeling of privilege and achievement from successfully flying a loop.

I am convinced that learning the technique for flying a loop improved my confidence and competence as a private pilot. I still benefit from my foray into aerobatics.

Spreading My Wings

The two or three years from 1991 were a bit of a honeymoon period in my life as a pilot. I just wanted to fly as often as I could, and as far as I could, to gain experience of flying in as many aircraft types as possible. And between flights, I had to go to work and wanted to spend time with my family. The trick was to combine flying with either of those. I often entertained clients by taking them on aerial sight-seeing tours.

At about this time, SL was doing a lot of work for Carrier Engineering – the name has changed several times since then. We completed several good-sized insulation projects for the company, which was based in a large industrial unit just opposite the airfield at Biggin Hill. Carrier manufactured huge refrigeration skids – essentially, a large steel frame with extremely low temperature plant fitted to it. These were used in the petrochemical industry around the world, from Norway to Brazil.

I invited two of the project managers from Carrier to join me for a flight and arranged to meet them at King Air, after work at five o'clock. After signing my guests into the flying club, I collected the keys for the plane and we walked to the air side of the building where the GA7 Cougar twin G HIRE was parked. I was becoming used to carrying out the normal check-out procedures whilst explaining what I was doing. Then, once we were on board and safely belted into our seats, I would tell them about the etiquette of radio communication and what happens prior to take off and during the flight.

At the hold, with permission from the tower to line up on the runway, once I was given clearance to take off, I applied full power. G HIRE would accelerate rapidly along the runway until we were looking upwards at the blue sky, leaving the ground and any thoughts of work below us. I always tried to take passengers flying on clear, sunny days, which made the experience all the more pleasant and memorable.

From Biggin Hill I would usually head north towards Blackheath, which is as close to central London as a private light aircraft is permitted to fly, unless the circumstances are exceptional. I would then turn east towards Kent. Provided they were not located beneath controlled air space, I would fly at fairly low altitude above my guests' homes. This went down well, especially if they hadn't previously seen their houses and gardens from above.

Back at Biggin Hill, I would often visit a small bar, just a short walk from the flying club apron, where their aircraft were parked overnight. The bar was accessible from the air side, so it was ideal to be able to leave the aircraft and go straight to the bar for a beer with my guests, and review the flying experience we had just shared. It was a watering hole with oodles of character and can best be described as a modern-day homage to the drinking club or bar of the Second World War era, but without the excitement of bombs dropping all around us.

Most of the customers were either pilots or people with a keen interest in aviation. Much like a golf club, where the talk is mostly about golf, the main topic of conversation in the bar was aviation.

There were all sorts of aviation memorabilia on the walls, and even hanging from the ceiling of the bar. One artefact that particularly intrigued me was an old Martin-Baker ejector seat, placed strategically to one side of the seating area. A padded-out fast jet flying suit complete with flying boots, was suspended above it, as if the occupant of the seat had just been ejected and crashed through the ceiling. My guests were amused, and invariably commented on this 'art installation' when they first visited the bar.

Holding my private pilot's licence enabled me to combine my passion for flying with business entertaining and sometimes travelling to site. Perfect. This became common knowledge among people in our industry; consequently, I acquired another nick name. At trade association events I was often referred to as *Biggles*. What else?

Any amount of mickey-taking or teasing about my passion for flying has no effect on me. Most men know that when you have the mickey taken out of you by your respected peers, this should be interpreted as a compliment, rather than an insult. This social behavioural trait seems to be uniquely British.

Americans are baffled by the way the depth of the friendship between men can be judged by the level of the insult you can hurl at a friend without giving offence. I recall seeing an episode of *Have I Got News for You* during which the American comedian Reginald D Hunter said exactly that.

5

Flying for Pleasure and More

'Never be too proud to turn back.
There are old pilots and bold pilots, but no old, bold pilots.'

Sandown Safeway

Back in 1991, as well as owning SL, Stan and I were directors of an engineering company. Unfortunately, the experience of part-ownership of this company was not all rosy, but I won't use this book to whinge about the challenges and pitfalls of engaging in light engineering. One of the roles I had in the engineering company was that of sales director. This was also my main role within SL. I have always loved being in sales. I find it such a challenge and I have to win. When I go into a project office that I have never visited before, my sole purpose is selling our services. I am intent on convincing them that my company is not only the best one to work with, but also that they would be remiss if they engaged another company.

At this time during the nineties, before the availability of such things on the internet, I used a printed publication called *Glenigan Sales Leads*. Published fortnightly, Glenigan listed all types of construction and engineering projects going on across the UK. I used to make contact with the project manager listed in Glenigan, and try to obtain the enquiry for any of their engineering requirements within the overall project.

I noticed there was a Safeway store being built in Sandown on the Isle of Wight. I phoned up the site office, and asked if there were any engineering packages within the construction contract for which our company could quote. We undertook engineering for the construction industry, manufacturing weather louvres, acoustic louvres, silencers and brise soleil. I had a productive telephone conversation with the friendly project manager, who told me there was a weather louvre package up for grabs, but as we were based in north Kent it might be a problem to return the tender by the deadline, which was three o'clock the next day. He also mentioned, as this was August and holiday high season, the chances of getting a ferry crossing were slim.

To get to Sandown from the offices of SL is a two-and-a-half-hour drive to Portsmouth, followed by a ferry crossing to Ryde, and another hour's drive to the Safeway construction site.

I responded confidently, 'No problem, we'll be there in the morning, and fax a quote over by three o'clock.'

The project manager agreed to let us quote for the package and explained how to find the construction site. Immediately, I telephoned King Air at Biggin Hill, and booked G BRRM, a Piper PA 28 160 HP low-wing plane.

My fellow director of the engineering company was Ray Ellis. Ray and I got on very well, partly because Ray was also a petrol-head. His hobby was racing modified saloon cars at tracks around the UK, including Brands Hatch, Snetterton, and Thruxton.

I went into Ray's office and told him, 'We've got an appointment tomorrow. You and me are going to fly to the Isle of Wight, to measure up for some louvres in a Safeway store. Meet me here in the morning.'

Ray and I drove together to Biggin the next morning and took off in Romeo Mike at 11:30. The flight to the Isle of Wight lasted around fifty minutes. The route took us over Mayfield in Sussex, then over the Sussex Downs. We flew overhead Shoreham Airport, communicating with Shoreham ATC, then over Thorney Island and Hayling Island, heading off over the sea towards the Isle of Wight.

This was just what I had imagined when I first started flying; using my pilot's licence for business on a legitimate tax-deductible flight. During our journey, we saw a Second World War gun emplacement in the Solent, now abandoned, from about 1500 feet. We also saw several ferries and many leisure craft in the Solent, travelling between the island and the mainland.

Once over the island, and in the vicinity of Sandown, I asked Ray to help me by looking out for the airfield. Locating a grass airfield nestling amongst green fields is not the easiest task in the world. This was also my first trip to the Isle of Wight. Ray had borrowed Stan's video recorder to record some of the trip. Once we had been circling in the area near Sandown Airport for about five minutes, I was starting to get annoyed with myself for not spotting the field. Ray was enjoying videoing everything from the air, including that Second World War gun emplacement in the Solent.

Tersely, I spoke to Ray through gritted teeth, 'Can you stop bloody videoing, and help me find the airfield?'

I must have sounded like John Cleese's absurdly comical character, Mr Stimpson, berating his teenage pupils in the 1986 film *Clockwise*. We looked at each other for a second and both burst out laughing. It did sound like I was telling off a naughty boy.

I'm glad to say, shortly after my Mr Stimpson moment, the runway came into view. A very clean approach and smooth landing followed. We taxied to the parking area for visiting aircraft, and exited Romeo Mike. I walked over to the tower to pay our landing fee. Ray told me that, on our final approach to the runway, whilst I was concentrating on getting us safely onto terra firma, he had noticed the site we were due to visit, not far from the airfield.

Ray and I walked briskly to the Safeway site, which took us about ten minutes. We reported to the project office. After the usual introductions, we went on to site, and I helped Ray take the measurements to compile our tender. After we had all the information that we required to submit a quote, we sought out the project manager and told him we were leaving, and returning to Kent. Now came the good part.

He escorted us to the car park on the way out and asked, 'Where is your car?'

I replied, 'Oh, we didn't come by car, I flew us in from Biggin Hill. We're now going back to the airport to have some lunch, then we'll fly back to Kent. You'll have your quote by three o'clock.'

The look on his face was priceless. I thanked him for his time, and we walked briskly along the narrow road back to the airfield, leaving a dumbfounded Safeway project manager.

Ray and I had an enjoyable lunch at Sandown, during which he worked out the cost of the work we had measured. We then phoned our office, where the quotation was rapidly typed up and faxed to the project manager to meet his three o'clock deadline.

I am pleased to recall that our tender was successful. The louvres were soon manufactured, painted and taken to site, to be fitted on the store which is now a Morrisons supermarket. Our louvres are probably still there today.

As a treat, when we departed Sandown Airport, I flew at low level, but above 500 feet, across the island, taking in Cowes from the air, as well as Shanklin and Ventnor. When we arrived back at the office it was around 16:45. Ray and I had a laugh about the day. I still have the video he took during our flight, including the recording of me asking him to assist with finding the 'bloody runway' at Sandown.

Twin to Le Touquet

Monday, 10th February 1992

Throughout 1991 and 1992, I was steadily building up my flying hours. I was alternating between flying the Cessna 172, and the trusty GA7 Cougar. When flying the twin, you cannot help but adopt an air of self-importance, tinged with superiority, when walking to the aircraft. Especially when others are checking out much smaller aircraft. Even more so when you are taxiing to the live runway prior to take-off, with both the engines roaring and straining to hurtle you into the air on your next adventure.

Speaking of adventures, the first time I took Stan for a flight in the Cougar was early in the year. We both drove to Biggin where G HIRE was waiting for us. We took off at 11:40, after filing our flight plan, and travelled the route to Le Touquet via Lydd. Stan was suitably impressed with having two engines propelling us through the skies of Kent, towards the coast. We called up Lydd ATC and requested an overhead flight en route, at an altitude of 3000 feet.

When cruising at 140 KIAS the Cougar is so stable that it gives the impression of driving on tarmac. With G HIRE trimmed out for straight and level flight, there was plenty of time for me to enjoy the flight too. I never tire of seeing the landscape and seascape from the air. I still find it fascinating to see so many large ships in the Channel. Container ships, tankers, and the specially designed car transporters that look like great big bricks in the water, with the stern hardly distinguishable from the bow. Their only purpose is to haul finished motor cars from Japan and Korea to European and UK ports, fulfilling the ever-increasing demand for shiny new cars.

It is remarkable how many vehicles these vessels can transport, ploughing through the sea, creating quite a wake as they go. The decks are adjustable so there is little wasted headroom, inside they are a bit like a multi-story car park. I have often stood on the south bank of the Thames at Gravesend and watched with incredulity as they disgorge their cargo on the north bank, at Tilbury Docks.

We called up Le Touquet when about five miles from the airfield, clearly visible across the Channel. I reported our position, number of souls on board, and expected time of arrival (ETA). Armed with the information we needed, the runway in use, QFE, wind speed and direction, provided by LFAT approach, and we continued.

By now I had established the plane in a shallow descent to our circuit height of 1000 feet. With variable pitch propellers on the Cougar, you can push the nose down, increasing the air speed considerably but not over-revving the engine, and still maintain the same revolutions per minute.

This is similar to when you return home from holidays in Italy or Spain, when the captain talks to his passengers over the PA system and says: 'We are just overhead Paris, and are starting our descent to Gatwick.'

He is doing much the same, by throttling back a little, thereby saving fuel, but increasing air speed courtesy of gravity.

Now I have to be truthful, because I am not the sort of pilot to never admit a mistake. There is no point, you're only deluding yourself if you don't recognise you've done something wrong, and hence you won't learn from it, and become a better pilot.

So, the remainder of the flight went like this. I established G HIRE on the downwind leg of the circuit; or I should say, I established G HIRE on the *wrong* downwind leg direction. Stan and I, in a twin-engine aircraft, were now hurtling at about a hundred knots, effectively *the wrong way along a one-way street*, at a thousand feet above the level of the airfield.

Fortunately, I realised my mistake quickly, before there were any other aircraft in the circuit, coming towards us in the opposite direction. Immediately I put Romeo Echo into a steep turn, at full power, and flew away from the circuit, in the direction of Hardelot, and the sand dunes.

Those dunes streaked below us. This was exciting stuff I must admit, albeit I shouldn't have been where I was, but quick thinking soon resolved the situation. Le Touquet tower kept calling up; they had expected me to be communicating when I was established downwind. Rather than tell them what had really happened, I called up approach, said in my best cool Captain Two Voices. 'Sorry about that, we had a temporary problem with transmission on the radio. I believe all is OK now. We will report when established down-wind.' ATC replied from the control tower in a strong French accent, but speaking clear English: 'Roger, Romeo Echo, report downwind.'

I was thinking, 'Phew, I got away with that.'

Needless to say, I did join downwind, but this time in the right direction, then reported finals to land, with three greens, and made a really smooth landing on their gloriously flat, very long concrete runway. Once our speed had decreased, I took the exit from the active runway, and noted on my knee pad the instructions given to me for the parking space where I was to bring G HIRE to a halt.

When you are taxiing a twin, it is easier to steer than a single-engine aircraft. With a single-engine, you steer using the toe brakes, to turn left you stop the left wheel from turning by pressing down on the left toe-brake, so the plane will move to the left.

However, with a twin, you still use the toe brakes, but to help the aircraft move in the intended direction, you push the left toe-brake simultaneously with applying more power to the right engine. In conjunction with the left wheel being slowed, the right engine is providing more forward thrust than the left engine, so it's possible to turn very accurately.

We were given a parking space on the apron in front of the control tower. We locked up the plane, and phoned for a taxi to take us into the town of Le Touquet. It's funny when I think of it now; during that trip and every subsequent visit to Le Touquet, Stan would visit a posh French lingerie shop in the street that led to the sea front to buy his wife Gloria a pair of silk pyjamas. I often wonder if she still has any of them?

Not Ostend but Dieppe

Monday 31st August 1992

Another memorable flight in a GA7 Cougar, but this time in G PLAS, happened in late summer, a time when the weather can be stormy and change rapidly.

There was supposed to be a mass fly-out to Ostend. I had never visited Ostend airfield and was ever keen to discover new airfields, and fly further afield. I was told by Elly, when I bumped into her at King Air, that there was a fly-out planned by the instructors, and their respective students, to fly en-masse to Ostend for lunch, stay for a couple of hours, then return. Would I fancy going along, in G PLAS, the second of the two Cougars King Air had available?

The fly-out was planned to depart in the early morning. I had booked G PLAS for the day. Elly asked if she could bring one of her friends for the ride.

Pat Simon, a friendly woman, with a lovely soft southern Irish accent, was a GP living in Kent at that time. I'm not sure if Pat still lives in Kent now; I haven't seen her for many years. I turned up at King Air with my wife, Jean, and met Elly, who introduced Pat.

Unfortunately, the weather at Biggin Hill that August Monday was not good for flying, with low cloud and some rain. After some deliberation, the King Air instructors, who were accompanying their students, decided it wasn't safe for them to fly. The students were at various stages of the PPL syllabus and flying either Cessna 152 or 172 aircraft. So, the plans for a mass fly-out to Ostend were scrapped. We were disappointed that rain seemed to have stopped fun for the day.

For readers who haven't had the pleasure of meeting Elly Blanche, to say that she is a highly competent pilot, instructor and examiner, is like saying Lewis Hamilton can drive a car quite well.

When Elly told us that the fly-out was off, she followed up with a suggestion: 'However, if you would still like to fly somewhere today, I've checked the Met for the weather; it's not so bad once we get further into Kent, and we can climb higher to miss some of the weather. It's looking like it should be better in France, so if you are still keen to fly, we could file a flight plan for Dieppe.'

As we would have two engines thrusting us through the elements, me with my IMC rating, and Elly with her several thousands of hours of experience, I jumped at the opportunity. 'Great, let's file our flight plan, then.'

I am not sure whether Pat and Jean were both as keen to fly as me, but neither of them refused. So, we departed Biggin Hill at 10:25 from runway 21. Shortly after take-off, we entered thick cloud.

We were soon on a south-easterly heading, taking us towards the Lydd VOR. I have to admit during the flight there was a lot of turbulence. However, I was using steely concentration to fly G PLAS on instruments, so it didn't register that the passengers in the back might be getting jittery. Meanwhile, Elly was ensuring that we were tuned to the correct frequencies, so that I could track towards and away from the VOR beacons along our route.

As I have said before, I really do get a buzz when flying on instruments, especially for real, as it was that day, rather than wearing foggles to simulate IMC conditions. It gives a tremendous feeling of satisfaction when flying accurately on instruments. It's both reassuring and immensely helpful to have someone as experienced as Elly sitting next to you, taking much of the stress out of the situation by doing the radio work. This allowed me to concentrate on keeping the plane straight and level, and on the correct heading and height.

At one point in the journey, Elly said: 'Les, have a quick look at the screen.'

It was late August, but the cloud we were travelling through had enough water in it, and the temperature was low enough, for there to be a deposit of icy slush on the nacelle, and on the windscreen.

After a quick glance up, I just kept on scanning the artificial horizon (AI), direction indicator (DI) VOR, altimeter, and air speed indicator (ASI). Our speed was around 140 knots, so we made rapid progress through the clouds over Kent. When scanning the instruments in IMC conditions, you always start with the AI, then scan another instrument, but immediately return to the AI. This is to make sure that you are keeping the wings straight and level, neither banking nor descending.

Eventually, when we were nearing mid-Channel, we popped out of the cloud, as if we had passed through a wall into bright sunshine, with a bright, blue sky in front of us, going on forever, across Europe. Well, over France, at least.

I am sure you can imagine the relief of the passengers sitting in the rear of the four-seat Cougar to suddenly see a wonderful, blue summer sky, and feel the warmth of the sun through the rear windows of Alpha Sierra. Later, we were told that Pat and Jean had not been happy during the turbulence, and were becoming increasingly scared by what they could NOT see. In IMC conditions there is nothing except the enveloping cloud visible through the window. When we eventually landed at Le Touquet, Pat resorted to self-medication with paracetamol and strong coffee to combat her stress headache.

We had to land at Le Touquet to clear customs and passport control, as Dieppe did not have an operational douane that day. We took off again, destination Dieppe. The route to Dieppe from Le Touquet is enchanting, with rolling countryside to the left, and the blue waters of the Channel to the right.

On reaching the airfield, which is a few miles inland from the coastal town and fishing port of Dieppe, we called up their approach radio frequency, but received no reply. I tried several times to make contact, but each time we received no response.

In this circumstance, the procedure is to fly overhead the airfield at a safe height, to see if there is any activity on the ground, or in the vicinity. By calling up on the approach frequency and making several blind calls other aircraft operating in the area tuned to that frequency will hear you, and will note your intentions. You also listen for the radio calls of other aircraft.

When you get a chance to do so, it is great to be able to fly low legally; in this instance, at around 500 feet above the runway. With the wheels down, and the nose up, it enables slow flight, for the pilot to decide the direction to land, to assess the condition of the runway and check for potential hazards when landing.

We made several blind calls, and made a few low approaches of the runway. I needed to see which way the wind sock was pointing, giving a visual cue to the runway to use for landing. After we agreed which runway to use, and that there was no conflicting traffic, I approached low over some fields with grazing livestock, and made a very smooth landing.

Elly commented on the landing; I always felt I had to fly extra well if my GFT examiner was sitting next to me. We taxied to the parking area, exited Alpha Sierra, and headed off to get a taxi into Dieppe for lunch.

The following account is taken from an article I wrote and had published in *Pilot*, Britain's best-selling general aviation magazine, describing my first experience of visiting Dieppe.

Pilot, October 1992 edition

We left the aircraft, and walked to the bar / lounge, at the side of the apron. Inside were two Brits, waiting for a hole in the weather across the Channel so they could navigate their Luscombe (High wing, two-seat vintage aircraft) back to England. I asked where everyone was, and was told they'd gone to lunch, they passed on a message for any visiting pilots: 'If you want any refreshments etc. help yourself and leave the money on the counter. If you need a taxi, you can use the telephone.' Can you imagine this anywhere else?

After a very pleasant lunch in Dieppe, we returned to the airfield, now completely deserted. The weather was CAVOK and the Luscombe was probably at its home airfield by now.

I started to carry out the pre-flight checks, when an old Volvo drove up to the control tower, a smiling leather-jacket-clad French controller / airfield manager walked over and introduced himself. I explained about our earlier blind calls and overhead passes, and he confirmed the lunch theory.

He invited me over to the tower to file our flight plan for our direct return to Biggin Hill, and said he'd contact Le Touquet and tell them we were going back direct, and would I like him to wait for thirty minutes before he sent the flight plan, so we could have a coffee before we left. I thanked him, but said we'd leave as soon as our checks were complete, 'Oh by the way, how much do I owe you for the landing fee?' I enquired. 'It is a public holiday in France, no charge today, have a safe flight and look forward to seeing you again.'

After obtaining clearance to take off, we headed straight back across the Channel towards Beachy Head, which was by now reflecting the sun, some sixty miles away.

What a memorable day that was. I do not know of any other airfields where twins do not get charged for landing, or where you may help yourself to refreshments and are trusted to leave payment at the counter. So, if you have not yet visited Dieppe airfield, I can thoroughly recommend it.

Porsche 911 Carrera Targa – my pride and joy in the mid-eighties.

Margaret Butler and me, at the King Air Christmas party. Margaret was my PPL instructor, and the Chief Flying Instructor and co-owner of King Air, Biggin Hill.

CERTIFICATE OF
FIRST
SOLO FLIGHT

It is hereby recorded that _LES HOMEWOOD_

on _22nd AUGUST 1989 AT REDHILL_

did command a motorised, heavier than air object, namely an aeroplane, in the skies
above Biggin Hill and did with auspicious airmanship, and with due regard to fellow
aviators, take off the said aeroplane, from runway _36_.... and did return successfully to
that same runway, in that same aeroplane, after one complete circuit of the aerodrome,
without the aid of an instructor or any other person, passenger, automatic device or
mirrors so far as could be observed from the ground.

Henceforth, the bearer of this certificate will be entitled to append after his name the
worthy title of Air Captain (Elect) of the Biggin Aeroplane Student Elite or

A.C. (E) of the B.A.S.E.

The bearer will further be entitled to approach the clubhouse bar with a nonchalant
swagger, double vision, uncontrollable shakes and a silly grin and offer drinks all round.

Very well done _Margaret Butler_ .... INSTRUCTOR

Congratulations .... CHIEF FLYING INSTRUCTOR

King Air School of Flying

This certificate was presented to me by Margaret Butler after completing my first solo flight. Although
the wording is humorous, it marks the first significant milestone in the student's path to achieving
their goal of holding a Private Pilot's Licence. As such it also motivates.

Cessna 152 Aerobat G BOYA and me, after I had completed my first solo flight.

Celebratory champagne and cake at my company office, on the day that I passed my General Flight Test, and qualified as a private pilot.

Piper Cadet G KDET and me. I used G KDET to take my parents, Pat and Eric Homewood, for their first flight in a light aircraft, over Kent and south-east London in 1991.

Elly and me, beside G BOOL at LFAT Le Touquet Airfield after my check-out in a four-seat Cessna 172 and my first cross-Channel flight. I completed several touch-and-go circuits, before we eventually landed at Le Touquet and headed into the town for lunch.

On the apron, air-side at Biggin Hill. I also flew another GA7, G HIRE.

My trial lesson in G ROLO, a Robinson R 22, with John Dines. May Day 1994 at Redhill Aerodrome. A breathtaking experience and a memorable birthday gift from my wife, Jean.

Grumman American AA5 B Tiger, G TYGA. A tiger, by name and by nature, it was sporty in the air, and manoeuvrable on the ground.

View from inside Heathrow Airport Terminal 4, August 1991.

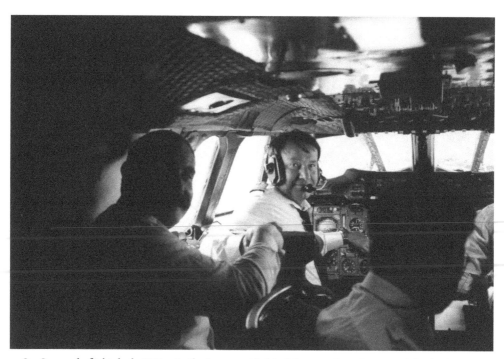

On Concorde flight deck. Sitting in the jump seat behind the captain, prior to push back via a tug.

Jean and Les enjoying the flight. Notice how narrow Concorde was compared with other passenger jet aircraft.

Cessna 172 G AWCN, the Reims Rocket, was built in 1968 and had a variable pitch propellor. This combined, with an engine with lots of grunt, made it a safe and stable aircraft to use when flying with four adults up.

Short final approach, to land, runway 20 at Rochester.

Steep turn over Bodiam Castle, Sussex.

Toby in the foreground, with his brother Oliver, ready for their first flight with me as pilot in control.
Circa 2012

A nerve-wracking flight, with such precious cargo on board.

G-TUKE at Headcorn Lashenden.

October 1995. Antonov AN 2 OM-UIN on the grass runway at Headcorn Aerodrome.

The cockpit and controls of Captain James Black's Antonov AN 2, OM-UIN.

Certificate of Flight

This certifies that

......Lee..R..Homewood.

has flown the Antonov AN-2 biplane

on ....7..October..1995....

at ......Headcorn.........

Signed ...James Black...........

Aerobatics International Ltd., 2 Brookside, Hatfield, Hertfordshire AL10 9RR

Certificate of my flight in the Antonov AN 2 biplane.

At Redhill Aerodrome, waiting for the propellor to be spun by hand to start the engine.

Leeds, Deal and Dover Castles in Kent, and Bodiam Castle in East Sussex. Photographs were taken at various times of day by family and friends during pleasure flights above Kent and East Sussex.

Deal Castle.

Dover Castle.

Bodiam Castle.

Turner Contemporary, an art gallery adjacent to Margate beach, in Kent was designed by David Chipperfield, and opened in 2011.

The 'National Memorial to the Few' at Capel-le Ferne, Kent, is dedicated to the heroic and selfless deeds of the men who won the Battle of Britain.

Canterbury Cathedral, the mother church of the world-wide Anglican faith community.

Oil seed rape in bloom in the fields near the oyster hatchery and farm at Reculver, Kent.

An unprecedented experience to be able to fly over Gatwick Airport and see entire fleets of aircraft grounded, during the second Covid pandemic lockdown, May 2021.

06/05/2021

VOR beacon on the cliffs, St Margaret at Cliffe, near Dover.

August evening landing at Rochester, the cockpit instruments reflected in the window.

Coming in to land at Biggin Hill Airport on a misty afternoon. A little high, 4 white Papi's visible to the left of the runway threshold.

Shadow of Cessna 172 Skyhawk G-BYET during a late November afternoon landing at Rochester.

Upside down over Sussex, see the pilots rear view mirror, on top of the canopy.

My rearward view from the Spitfire. Beachy head by my left shoulder.

28th May 2021, celebrating my recent seventieth birthday. I'll never forget the flight in Spitfire MKTR9 G-ILDA at Boultbee Flight Academy. Pilot, John Gowdy to my left, with ground crew, Simon, to John's left.

The world turned upside down.

6

Something Fast, Something Big and Something Different

'To most people the sky is the limit.
To those who love aviation, the sky is home.'

Concorde

➤ In the United States of America, Queen Elizabeth II was the guest of George H W Bush, and during her state visit she became the first British monarch to address the US Congress.

➤ In Moscow, the Soviet parliament approved a law allowing its citizens to travel abroad.

➤ Deep beneath the English Channel, the breakthrough of the North Rail Tunnel between England and France occurred.

➤ In Kent the M20 motorway was opened, providing a motorway link between London and Dover, three years in anticipation of the opening of the Channel Tunnel.

➤ In the Netherlands, Manchester United won the European Cup Winners' Cup, beating Barcelona 2 – 1 in Rotterdam.

➤ In England, for a record eighth time, Tottenham Hotspur won the FA Cup. They beat Nottingham Forest 2 – 1 at Wembley.

➤ And in East Farleigh, Les Homewood was forty years old.

For three or four years during my late thirties, I threw at least one large party a year. The house where we lived was perfect for entertaining. Most of our friends were a bit older than me and we had attended their fortieth birthday celebrations, so they assumed whenever I was giving a party, that I was also celebrating a milestone birthday. At least one person would give me a fortieth birthday card.

This amused my eldest daughter, Claire, who pointedly asked, 'Dad, when are you going to be forty? You seem to have been thirty-nine for years.'

When my birthday eventually rolled around and my fortieth birthday party took place in May 1991, it was quite a party, with around 120 guests, dancing and having fun.

Before the big party, Jean and I had dinner alone in the restaurant at the Tudor Park Hotel in Bearsted, just east of Maidstone. We often used this hotel and were friendly with both the maître-d and the head waiter. We enjoyed the meal, as usual, and after dessert the head waiter brought a small cake to mark my birthday, and we all raised a glass.

Jean reached into her handbag and pulled out an envelope printed with my name. She handed it to me. Opening it with some trepidation, because I was not expecting anything like this to happen, I took out a printed voucher and read the message, which began something like: '*Congratulations on your 40th birthday. You have been given a trip for two to fly to Paris on Concorde…*'

I must admit, for once I was speechless. To say it was a surprise is an understatement. Without my knowledge, Jean had organised this, and paid for it. We were going to fly to Paris Charles De Gaulle airport, on Concorde, stay for two nights in a Paris hotel, and then return on an Airbus, which in 1991 was a comparatively new type of passenger jet. I don't remember the exact dates of our trip because it's not recorded in my log book, but I am sure it was early August. Trips in Concorde were very popular, and fully booked well in advance.

I used to buy two flying magazines each month, *Pilot*, and *Flyer*. In one of these publications, I had read an article submitted by a PPL who had been a passenger on a Concorde flight the year before. In advance of his check-in at Heathrow Airport, he had contacted the head office to ask if he could sit in the jump seat on the flight deck for take-off.

He was a very lucky man, and was permitted to experience take-off whilst sitting on the flight deck of this passenger-carrying fighter jet. On most big jet aircraft there is a small seat that folds out from the bulkhead of the aircraft. It's there so that a senior instructor or flight engineer can observe the flight and assess the crew doing their job, or witness the performance of the aircraft. They can see exactly what is happening throughout the flight.

Armed with the information I had read in the magazine, I called up the flight operator, Air France, and spoke to one of the staff involved with the administration of celebration flights, as they came to be known. I recounted the article and asked if I could sit on the jump seat for take-off. The PPL sharing his experience with the aviation community must have flown with British Airways, as Air France were unaware of this happening on any of their aircraft.

The Air France administrator did not dismiss my request and said, 'Thank you for calling us, Mr Homewood. We will contact the captain, nearer the departure date, and ask on your behalf. It will be his decision on the day.'

I thanked her for listening to my request, and assured her, whatever the captain decided, just to be flying in Concorde, sitting in the cabin with the other ninety-nine passengers will be the thrill of a lifetime.

For those interested in statistics, Concorde had four jet engines, Rolls Royce/SNECMA Olympus 593s, each producing 38,000 pounds of thrust with reheat. Take-off speed was 250 mph, with a cruising speed of 1350 mph. Yes, that is one thousand, three hundred and fifty miles per hour, at a height of sixty thousand feet. That's more than eleven miles above the surface of the Earth, and approximately twenty thousand feet higher than today's long-haul and European passenger jets.

Eventually the day came for us to fly to Paris on the world's only supersonic passenger aeroplane. We drove to Heathrow on a Saturday morning. Our departure time was about midday. I am pleased to say that most people who were booked to fly in this modern-day marvel of aviation were smartly dressed, which added to the sense of occasion. I think I was the only man wearing a bow tie, which was a bit of a trademark of mine. I used to wear a bow tie to site meetings, as well as when entertaining clients.

We arrived at the Concorde lounge and check-in, where we were greeted by friendly and helpful ground crew, all sporting chic Air France corporate attire. We were served with delicious canapés and an abundance of champagne.

The Concorde lounge was buzzing. The soon-to-be passengers were either high with excitement, or filled with trepidation in anticipation of the supersonic flight they were about to experience. There were people of all ages, and for most it was a celebration of some kind. There were plenty of passengers flying on Concorde for a birthday treat, or anniversary celebration. No one was there just to get to Paris.

We spoke to a couple, probably in their late twenties. The young woman said she had won the whole experience in an office raffle. What a prize to win! However, she was evidently anxious and explained that she had never flown in a jet before. Can you imagine? You have never travelled in a passenger jet, then your first taste of flying is aboard the world's fastest passenger jet.

A French purser called Marcel went around the lounge and spoke to everyone individually and ensured we were all happy. Politely he asked for our names and ticked the list on his Air France clip board.

Apologetically he said, 'Mr Homewood, I understand that you asked if you could sit on the jump seat on the flight deck for take-off?'

I confirmed that I had indeed phoned the flight administrator to enquire whether this was possible.

Marcel continued, 'I am afraid the captain said he is too busy today, and regrets he won't be able to allow this.'

I replied, 'That's no problem, I'm more than happy to be in the cabin. I'm looking forward to the flight.'

I had already seen the plane from the window of the departure lounge, close enough to appreciate the distinctive profile with its beak-like drooping nose. I fancied that it was trying to look inside the building.

After a while the champagne glasses were taken from us, and we were led to the departure gate. Then via the flying bridge that enables passengers to enter the cabin directly from the departure gate we boarded Concorde. Marcel successfully shepherded us all on to the plane like a well-trained border collie.

Jean and I were the last to board. Jean walked just ahead of me. The chief stewardess spoke to Jean, 'This way madam,' and led her into the passenger cabin and I was just about to follow.

Marcel stopped to me, 'No, not you Mr Homewood,' he gestured to our left, pointed towards the flight deck, and with a beaming smile he announced, 'You are invited to sit on the flight deck for take-off.'

To access the flight deck, you have to shuffle through a very narrow passage. Once on the flight deck, each of the flight crew shook my hand, and welcomed me to their office. I can remember the captain was called Jean, and the first officer was Francois. I am annoyed that I can't recall the flight engineer's name.

They knew that I was a private pilot, and I'm sure they guessed that I was totally in awe of them. The captain pulled out a folding seat from the bulkhead just behind his own seat, then gestured to me to sit down. He passed me a head set, and showed me where to plug it in. With my seat belt secured, I could listen to all their pre-flight checks, and the chatter between Heathrow ATC and our Concorde. I regret not making a note of the call sign of the plane that I flew in that day. The experience was so immersive that it didn't occur to me to do so, for future reference thirty years on.

Anyway, there I was, pinching myself that I really was sitting on the flight deck of Concorde preparing for take-off. I watched and listened with intense interest as the crew communicated with one another and ATC. Soon it was time to start the engines, all four of them. Next, I felt the tug on the ground slowly push us backwards, then stop. Once the tug had disengaged from the nose wheel, this Air France Concorde, with one hundred passengers on board, started to taxi to the hold.

The captain said that we had been given priority for departure, so we overtook some ordinary passenger jets and a couple of jumbos, to be number one at the hold for runway 27, leaving towards the west.

The flight engineer advised me, 'You will need to lean forward, and hold on to the bar that is just below your seat to prevent you being forced too far back during take-off.'

After the engine performance instrument checks were completed, all four engines were unleashed and we started to roll. One-hundred-and-eighty tonnes of plane plus passengers accelerated until we reached the rotation speed, 250 miles per hour. The first officer, who was in control for this flight, under the captain's supervision, pulled back on the controls. The g-force pushing me back was incredible. Sitting on the jump seat, holding the bar, was only comparable to riding pillion on a Moto GP superbike, piloted by Valentino Rossi approaching the first bend of the Catalunya race track in Barcelona.

As we left the ground, the angle of climb felt insane. Not the gentle climb of today's passenger jets, this was more like a fighter being scrambled from an RAF base to intercept an aggressor.

After the initial climb, the captain turned around from his seat on the left-hand side and pointed to the vertical speed indicator, which was showing a climb rate of ten thousand feet a minute. Compare this with an Airbus A320, which would normally climb away at two thousand feet per minute, and it gives you an idea of the sheer power that those four Rolls Royce engines delivered.

We carried on climbing, then the captain operated the nose cone. It slowly rose, right there in front of me. A series of rather industrial-looking bolts whirred as it screwed itself on to the body of the plane around the windscreen. Concorde no longer had a droopy beak; it had morphed into a dart. It was apparent to me, sitting on the flight deck, just how small the windows were, with extremely limited views outside for the guys on the flight deck. Our flight continued over Wales and across the Irish Sea to the southern coast of Ireland. We had crossed Britain from east to west in less than fifteen minutes.

I suppose I was on the flight deck for about twenty minutes.

The captain said, 'I hope you enjoyed that,' and gave me one of his charts used during the flight as a souvenir.

Marcel suddenly appeared, still smiling, and showed me to my seat in the cabin, where Jean had been waiting patiently on her own.

Seated in the passenger cabin, I could see the digital speed indicator on the bulkhead recording 580, 600, 640, 700, 750 mph, then through the sound barrier. It was a euphoric experience to watch the digital speed display: 800, 900, 1000, increasing steadily to 1340 mph. The aircraft and we ordinary citizens were travelling faster than a bullet from of a rifle.

Whilst hurtling through the air at twice the speed of sound, the glamorous female cabin attendants were matching the speed of the plane with the fastest trolley service I have ever experienced. Air France in-flight catering was as spectacular as the aeroplane itself. The food was served on Raymond Loewy-designed white bone china tableware. Raymond Loewy-designed silver cutlery, crystalware and linen napkins completed each place setting, laid on white linen table mats that covered the deep tables, folded out over our laps from the seat in front. The tables were considerably larger than those encountered on today's jets. Concorde had only two seats either side of the aisle. And there was still more champagne, which we drank from the lead crystal glasses.

The interior of the passenger cabin of Concorde was surprisingly narrow. It is worth mentioning that the windows in the cabin were also considerably smaller than those in modern passenger jets. When I looked out skywards, the colour was a more intense deep blue than the colour you see out of the window of an Airbus. At sixty thousand feet you are on the edge of space. From Concorde's windows at this height, I could see the curvature of Earth below; something that I will never forget.

Our route continued from the southern tip of Ireland, over the Atlantic Ocean, across the Bay of Biscay, down towards Spain. Only because it was flying over the sea was Concorde permitted to pass through the sound barrier and achieve its maximum speed. The aircraft then reduced speed and turned inland over central France, on a north-easterly heading towards Paris Charles De Gaulle airport.

As we were flying towards Paris and gradually descending, all of us inside the cabin were able to appreciate the flight profile of Concorde on final approach. It has been captured on film so many times – the delta wings at an angle of attack of thirty degrees, with the nose cone down, allowing the flight crew some visibility out of the window. It was certainly impressive, viewed from inside the aircraft. As we were approaching to land, I am sure Parisians were looking up in admiration of this most elegant of elite aircraft.

To be honest, I don't remember much about the two night-stay in Paris. By far the most memorable part of the entire three days was the outward journey. Sadly, in today's economic climate and environmentally aware world, I don't believe anyone will ever again travel to their destinations across the globe as fast, as high, or in such style.

A Bigger Twin

Tuesday, 11th January 1994

The GA7 Cougar was not the only twin I have ever flown. In January of 1994, I had the opportunity to get at the controls of a Piper (PA 34) Seneca III. This model was introduced in 1981, built in the United States of America by Piper Aircraft. It was built primarily for business use.

G OMAR was owned by Dennis Hulme, a friend of a friend, as they say.

Dennis had gone to visit some relatives in Dinard in France. His Seneca was based at Redhill Aerodrome in Surrey. A good friend of Dennis was an instructor and instrument rated pilot called Islam. I am not sure if that was his first or second name, but everyone called him Islam.

Dennis and I had a mutual acquaintance, Fred Insole. Fred owned a few shops in Maidstone, but had also been a British Airways pilot. Fred asked me, on behalf of Dennis, if I would like to fly the Seneca to Dinard with Islam, who was going to collect him. Dennis had been suffering with some health problems for a while, which meant he had to fly with a safety pilot. He was not permitted to be in sole charge of the aircraft in flight. I contacted Islam, and he was already aware of the situation.

It had been raining heavily and almost continuously for weeks. Islam suggested we meet at Biggin Hill. Redhill has a grass runway. He was going to have to take off from one of the very narrow concrete taxi ways at Redhill, as it was impossible to use the water-logged grass runway. Islam wanted as little weight as possible in G OMAR, in order to be able to get airborne quickly from the taxi way.

I met Islam at Biggin Hill control tower building, where we cleared outbound customs. After a pre-flight briefing, I was allowed to occupy the captain's left-hand seat in Alpha Romeo. I then taxied to the hold for runway 21, where the usual pre-take off power checks are carried out. This Seneca was the first plane I would fly that had four passenger seats behind the two cockpit seats. The pairs of rear seats faced each other, two facing rearwards and two forwards, with a side door into the cabin, too. Somewhat like an old-fashioned railway carriage.

I was given the instruction to line up on the runway, then given clearance to take off. Immediately I noticed a remarkable difference in engine power when I compared the Seneca with the Cougar. With only 2000 rpm, after I let go of the toe brakes, Alpha Romeo shot along the runway, like a Top Fuel dragster at Santa Pod Raceway. The climb out from the runway was equally impressive.

Islam was the holder of a full instrument rating (IR) as airline pilots must have. We were given clearance to climb to ten thousand feet. We were going to fly in the airways, with the bigger commercial boys.

I kept back pressure on the controls and watched as we climbed through 3000, 4000, 5000 and on up to 10,000 feet. Once at our cruising altitude, Islam pointed out the switch for autopilot. I flicked the switch to the ON position, and then let go of the control yoke, and took my feet off the rudder pedals.

This was my first time flying at this height, in the controlled airways, and my first time flying on autopilot. It was incredible how still and smooth the journey was at this altitude on auto.

After a while we were contacted by ATC, and given another heading to fly, just like the jets that take you and me on our holidays. I wound in the compass heading, and the autopilot gently banked the aircraft, and the DI slowly rotated until we reached the new heading. The wings were then levelled, and we continued on our way. By now, we were looking down at the Isle of Wight from ten thousand feet. We were both just sitting there, sucking Trebor Extra Strong Mints, with our hands in our laps. All we had to do was to monitor the engines and keep a look for any conflicting traffic. I am glad to say, there was none that day.

After coasting out over the Needles, our route took us directly over the Channel, towards the islands of Jersey and Guernsey. Flying out over the sea at 10,000 feet is a very different sensation from cruising at heights between 1000 to 2400 feet around the south-east of England, which was my regular air space when visiting Headcorn and Lydd, or just out on a jolly.

Islam and I chatted during the rest of the flight, and he asked if I wanted to land Alpha Romeo at Dinard, our destination airfield. Obviously, I was eager to land this bigger twin. It felt so comfortable and stable to fly, as if I'd been at the controls several times before.

To land the Seneca III, you have very specific speeds to maintain on approach. Dinard is due south of Jersey, so with around five miles to run, after receiving approach and landing instructions from Dinard ATC, I set up G OMAR for a straight-in approach to the airfield. Landing flaps are selected on approach, with full flap selected on finals. The speed I had to maintain on initial final approach was 100 knots indicated air speed, then on short finals, an exact ninety-two knots had to be established, resulting in a speed of eighty-five knots on short finals to the threshold.

I found the final flare out on to the runway surprisingly easy, which pleased me, as I had a full instrument rated pilot sitting next to me, and wanted to demonstrate how well I could fly. The landing was very smooth – no bouncing. We PPLs always joke and say that if we bounce a couple of times, at least we only pay for one landing fee.

After the speed had decreased along the runway, I took the designated exit and taxied to the parking area, carried out magneto checks and shut the plane down.

I was very encouraged when I met Dennis Hulme for the first time in the terminal building. He had been watching his own aeroplane flying in. When I told him that I had been at the controls of G OMAR, and had landed his aeroplane, he was surprised. It had been landed so smoothly that he had assumed Islam was at the controls.

The return flight to Biggin was a totally different experience. As Dennis owned the aircraft, and he could only fly with a safety pilot beside him, I sat in the back, in the executive-style seating.

This was the first, and to date, the only time I have travelled in a plane with this seating configuration. It was quite a strange sensation, speeding along the runway, with my back to the engine, as they say on the railways.

When G OMAR rotated and took off, the acute angle of climb was all the more noticeable because I was looking back at the runway, as we were leaving the ground. On the climb away from Dinard, Islam had to intervene a couple of times whilst Dennis was at the controls. I could then appreciate the need for a safety pilot to fly beside him.

Redhill was the destination airport on our way back, as Alpha Romeo was hangered there. I had arranged for one of my staff to collect me from Redhill, and take me back to Biggin Hill, to collect my car.

That was another amazing flying experience, and a great memory.

Another aircraft type I've flown, and have recorded in my pilot's log book. If I never get a chance to do it again, at least I can say I flew a twin-engine aircraft in the UK air lanes, at 10,000, and on autopilot.

Endnote

Whilst carrying out research for this book I came across the Air Accident Investigation Board (AAIB) Field Investigation Report EW/G2001/4/1 in AAIB Bulletin No: 9/2001.

Just a few years after my flight in G OMAR, the aircraft came to a sad end. It was destroyed during a crash landing on 2nd April 2001.

Fortunately, no one was killed, although the pilot sustained some head injuries. There were no passengers. However, considerable damage was caused to a house and garden when the pilot made a forced landing short of the airfield at Shoreham by Sea.

The AAIB report states '*The roof collapsed absorbing much of the aircraft's forward speed and the aircraft yawed left and slid into the rear garden of the house largely intact.*'

It was fortunate that there was no one working or playing in the garden when the plane came down.

The report concentrates on the fuelling of the aircraft. It is evident that human error in calculating the amount of fuel needed to complete the journey resulted in engine failure. The plane ran out of fuel. A salutary reminder to all who fly to check the fuel.

The Biggest All-Metal Biplane

Saturday 7th October 1995

During 1995 I received some correspondence from Headcorn Aerodrome informing me that Captain James Black, a senior British Airways pilot and an importer of the Antonov AN 2, would be visiting the airfield with an Antonov. I must admit that until I received the notification I had never heard of the type, let alone thought I would have the opportunity to fly one.

The correspondence was an invitation for three PPLs to pay £75 each and fly the AN 2 for 20 minutes, and for eleven passengers to fly for an hour, for £35 each. After reading the article, and looking at the photographs of the Antonov in flight, I made contact with Captain Black immediately and confirmed my keen interest to fly the aircraft.

I soon discovered that Antonov is a Ukrainian aircraft manufacturing and services company founded by Oleg Antonov in 1946. Antonov designed and built a wide range of aircraft during the Soviet era. The AN 2 was a mass-produced single-engine biplane that first flew in 1947 and was widely used to aid the post-war recovery of economies in the Soviet Block. Critics said that it looked archaic even in 1947.

The Antonov AN 2 was intended for both agricultural and military use, for everything from crop dusting, or transporting cargo and livestock, to dropping soldiers in hostile terrain. All were possible because of its remarkable durability and high lifting power, which have given the aircraft a long service life. It can to take off from and land in rough airfields – not just unpaved, grass airstrips, but dirt roads and forest clearings in the middle of Russia's sparsely settled wilderness. So, the grass runway at Headcorn would be no problem.

At this time, I was flying the GA7, the Cessna 172, and the French Aerospatiale Robin DR400 180 HP from both Biggin Hill and from Headcorn. The Robin was another great aeroplane to fly. It had a stick control like a jet fighter, rather than the yoke usually fitted in light aircraft, and passenger jets.

Outwardly, the Robin is a very pretty aeroplane, with a goldfish-bowl-like plexiglass canopy, which gives the best outward visibility of all aircraft, other than helicopters, and Tiger Moths that have no canopy at all. The

Robin is also a joy to fly, and as the stick control is so short, and positioned between your knees, when you need to turn, you seem to lean your body in the direction you want to go, and the plane leans over too. I must admit, the Robin is my all-time favourite plane to fly.

To return to the Antonov. I don't think it took James Black long to sell out the visit to Headcorn. It's an opportunity that came along infrequently in those days and I can't remember the last time I saw an Antonov available for PPLs to fly.

I received confirmation that my seat was booked for the plane's visit to Headcorn Lashenden on 7th October. I had told one of my neighbours in East Farleigh about the trip. He liked aeroplanes and bought a ticket to be a passenger.

We got to Headcorn at around 13:00 and had a cup of tea, whilst waiting for the Antonov to arrive from its home airfield of Blackbushe aerodrome in Surrey. Roy, my neighbour, and I, the other two PPLs and the rest of the passengers stood outside the control room at Headcorn, looking skyward to catch a first glimpse of this mammoth of the skies.

The ATC at Headcorn came out of his room, and said, 'It's just called up, and will be in the circuit in a few minutes.'

We looked towards the downwind for runway 28, and there it appeared, getting unbelievably bigger in the sky as it approached. Watching it turn on to base leg, and then finals, I think, to a man, we used all the descriptive words we knew and maybe a few expletives too, to describe the appearance of OM UIN.

We watched in awe as it lumbered slowly over the threshold of runway 28, rapidly lost speed and landed in a surprisingly short distance. Then it rumbled at low speed to the parking area for visiting aircraft at Headcorn, near the parachute club planes. With the 1010 horse power, nine-cylinder Shvetsov ASh-62 radial engine now quiet, and the four-bladed propellor static you could really appreciate the dimensions of this huge all-metal biplane.

James came over to the control room and chatted to the ATC for a while, then introduced himself to the group of PPLs and passengers waiting in anticipation of the flight. After his initial address to all, he took us three PPLs to one side, and gave a briefing on the procedures of flying the AN 2.

He then said, 'Now, who wants to be the first to fly?' To my surprise, the other two looked at their feet.

Or was it just that before they could answer I said, 'I'll go first.'

The other two did look relieved, though.

Soon the eleven passengers and the other two PPLs boarded the plane via a short aluminium ladder leant against to door opening. It all looked very utilitarian Eastern bloc.

Finally, I climbed on board along with James Black, who was going to operate the engine whilst I flew India November. As the AN 2 is a tail dragger, not a tricycle undercarriage, it has a nose-up angle on the ground, and walking to the flight deck is up a slope, with two steps up to get to the pilot's and first officer's seats.

I took my seat on the left, and secured my seat harness. From the captain's seat in the AN 2, you are about ten feet from the ground, like a World War Two bomber pilot preparing for take-off.

The yoke on the AN 2 is the size of a London bus steering wheel, cut in half. The rudder and foot brake pedals are like cut-down scaffold boards. The windscreen wraps around the flight deck, and is faceted like the pre-decimal three penny bit. I slid and closed the small captain's window. James started the enormous radial engine, which belched out a puff of exhaust, then roared into life, as loud as a bull elephant in musth.

James did the radio communication with Headcorn ATC, as I taxied very slowly to the hold for runway 28. I took the opportunity to glance behind me into the cabin. To see all those passengers looking at me was quite surreal. In just a few minutes, I was going to be flying them around the skies of Kent.

We completed the power checks at the hold for 28.

James said, 'Hold the controls fully back. It will lift quickly. As soon as you have a positive climb, which will happen quicker than you might expect, push the controls forward. Establish a lesser, but still positive rate of climb, and watch the speed increase.'

I lined up on the numbers of runway 28, held India November on the brakes, then James pushed the throttle and propellor levers fully forward. I held the controls fully back and off we all went, along the bumpy grass of Headcorn, which posed no problem to the AN 2. They can take off from rutted tracks in forest clearings or the grassy plains of the steppes.

As we climbed away from the airfield, I pushed the controls forward to maintain a safe speed, and avoid getting into a stall, which at low altitude could be very serious indeed. We continued upward, and levelled off at around 1500 feet.

Unlike flying in Cessnas, Pipers or Robins, you have to control the AN 2 all the time. You can't let go of the yoke, and reach behind to get a sandwich out of your flight bag, or open the chart to check where you are. It has to have continuous control inputs.

It was an amazing experience to be piloting the largest all-metal biplane in the world through the Kent air space, with thirteen passengers behind me. I couldn't help but look down at villages we passed, and wonder what the people on the ground were thinking as they saw and heard this enormous aircraft flying low over their heads.

My twenty minutes of flying the Antonov went very quickly, and on return to the circuit, I established India November on the downwind leg of the circuit, expecting James to takeover for the landing.

However, James said, 'On finals keep the speed to around fifty-five knots, and keep the nose up.'

I did exactly that, and concentrated intently on the final approach, not wanting to make a mess of the landing, after a successful take off and cruise. I kept watching the speed, all the time maintaining a nose-up attitude. We came in and landed exactly on the numbers of runway 28, and to be honest, to my surprise there was no bouncing along the runway.

As we slowed, I pressed down on the left rudder pedal, and pulled the left-hand brake lever on the yoke. It has one metal brake lever on either side of the control yoke, like old-fashioned bike brakes. Slowly, but surely, this Goliath turned to the left, and I continued to taxi back to the parking space designated for the Antonov's visit.

There were quite a lot of spectators at Headcorn that day, to see and photograph the visiting AN 2. As I taxied along, parallel to the runway, there were enthusiasts in the parking field on the other side of the fence taking photos. I wonder if anyone took any video. It would be good to have, as a reminder of the day.

We carried out the usual magneto checks before shutting down the engine. I slumped back in the seat, and looked across at James with a huge smile on my face.

James grinned and said, 'Well done, Les, that was very well flown.'

Once I had had my turn flying the AN 2, I went into the cabin and sat down next to one of the passengers, in the seat vacated by the next PPL whose turn it was to fly. He climbed his way up to the left-hand seat on the flight deck. So, now armed with the knowledge I had gained during my flight, I was keen to see how his handling of India November would be compared to mine.

To bring this chapter to an end. After the second take-off, flight and landing, the man sitting beside me spoke to me.

'Your landing was better than his.'

I had to agree. There had been a loud bang and a shudder as he put India November on the numbers of runway 28.

Some years after my flight, I read an article in Pilot magazine, about the Antonov AN 2, the heading of the article read 'Big, Heavy, Noisy and Fun'. Many people who know me well thought that was a good description of me too.

Tiger Moth

Saturday, 21st July 2001

Another memorable experience, and another birthday gift from my wife, was a flight in a de Havilland DH82A Tiger Moth, call sign G-AKUE. Jean knew it was the sort of present that would please me. I arrived at Redhill Airport that day with Jean, and our younger daughter, Katie, and reported to the office in the hangar where Kilo Echo was kept overnight. Fortunately for me, I just scraped under the maximum weight for take-off, which was sixteen stone, I have never been a skinny guy. Too much good living I suppose.

After my pre-flight briefing I was loaned a warm jacket, and flying helmet that had an in-built head set. I had told the pilot I held a PPL, and was keen to fly Kilo Echo.

As soon as I was firmly strapped into the front seat of the aircraft, a ground crew engineer spun the prop of G-AKUE and the engine burst into life, sending a great draft from the propeller back into my face, and swirling my big moustache around my face, tickling my nose.

Before the engine had started, the pilot in control had said to me, 'When in the air, due to the noise, it's difficult to hear through the head set, so when I waggle the joy stick, that's the sign for you to take control and fly the plane.'

We took off from the westerly runway, and climbed out over East Surrey Hospital, taking much the same route that I had taken on my first solo in 1989. The feeling of sitting in the front seat, with my head and shoulders outside in the fresh air, and being able to look all around and down with no plexiglass to impede my view was both primal and exhilarating. It gave me a real understanding of what it must have been like to be a pilot in the early years of flying, between the two world wars.

Once we reached some clear air space, in the vicinity of Oxted, the joy stick waggled so that was my cue. I started with a few slow banked turns, getting steeper and steeper all the time. This was a perfect gift. I could have stayed airborne flying that Moth for hours.

However, as with all commercially marketed 'birthday experiences', time was limited and my twenty minutes was all too soon over. The pilot in the rear seat resumed control of Kilo Echo. We side slipped on to the runway, as the Tiger Moth does not have flaps, or brakes come to that. He performed a text book landing, and we gradually came to a halt in his designated parking space on the airfield, where another lucky person was waiting for their chance to fly in this dream machine.

History of Tiger Moth: G-AKUE

I was told that the Tiger Moth I flew was manufactured in Portugal in 1939. The aeroplane was flown to Mozambique and then on to Northern Rhodesia where it was used for general transport. Many aircraft in the area were given names. This Tiger Moth was known as 'Nokomis, Daughter of the Moon', but to the local Africans it was simply known as 'The Big Bird'. Eventually the aircraft found its way to England.

Whilst completing research for this book I discovered that the British registration G-AKUE was allocated to a Tiger Moth on 12th February 1986.

The aircraft underwent a rebuild in 1988, then on 2nd January 1989, during take-off from Bryngwyn Bach Farm, near St Asaph's in Wales, it crashed on the edge of a field. The pilot had minor head injuries but the passenger sustained severe leg and other injuries. The aircraft was destroyed.

Presumably the aircraft was rebuilt or the registration was allocated to another Tiger Moth, because the plane in which I flew was operating from Redhill in 2001 and continued to do so until disaster struck yet again.

On 15th August 2010, G-AKUE had a slow speed collision with a Cessna 152, whilst on the ground and was damaged beyond repair. Fortunately, neither of the pilots were injured.

Endnote

Originally developed from the de Havilland DH60M Gipsy Moth, the DH82A Tiger Moth first flew in Oct 1931 and was put in production throughout the British Empire where it found many applications. Most notably it became the basic trainer aircraft for the RAF.

Around 8700 Tiger Moths were manufactured with 4200 being bought by the RAF; it remained in operational service until 1951. Throughout the war years this was the simple aircraft in which most RAF pilots learnt to fly.

The Tiger Moth saw service with university air squadrons, for glider towing duties, and as an aerobatic aeroplane at air shows.

This lovable aircraft continues to delight aviation and flying enthusiast. There are still around 250 operational Tiger Moths being used by private individuals and flying clubs.

Something Completely Different

Sunday 1st May, 1994

I drove to Redhill Aerodrome in Surrey with some of my family for a trial flying lesson in a helicopter. I had often said I would like to try flying a helicopter, so my wife Jean bought the lesson for me, to celebrate my birthday. Although my birthday falls in the middle of May, we took the opportunity to book the lesson on the Sunday of a Bank Holiday weekend, to make a family day of it.

The Cab Air office was below the control tower at Redhill. I went in and introduced myself. The thirty-minute lesson included some pre-flight briefing, so my airborne time was probably around eighteen to twenty minutes in reality. My instructor was a confident, fifty-something, ex-Fleet Air Arm pilot called John Dines. He told me he had more than 10,000 hours flying helicopters.

John explained the basic dynamics of helicopter flying to me in the training room, using a radio-controlled helicopter (not running) to describe the basic movement inputs required to fly. After the briefing, it was time for the real thing, so we strode out to a small apron, behind the control tower, where G ROLO, a Robinson R 22 two-seat helicopter was waiting for us.

The R 22 really is the Smart car of helicopters. A very snug two seats inside the cockpit with a single control column, which the occupant of either seat can access via a tee-bar configuration. I sat on the right-hand seat, which, unlike a fixed-wing aircraft, is the captain's seat. John started up the single-engine above us, and explained each of the instruments, and the temperatures and pressures the engine had to reach as it warmed up.

He then engaged the rotor above us, which soon began to rotate so fast it looked like a disc of haze over our heads. John demonstrated to me the helicopter-equivalent of moving the ailerons before flight in a fixed-wing. As he pushed the cyclic stick forward and back, and side to side, so the disc changed its orientation. It was fascinating to experience this for the first time.

Eventually, when he was satisfied with the engine performance instruments, he lifted the collective lever, between two seats This lever resembles the hand brake in a car. The power from the engine was transferred to the rotors, which in turn gave lift, and up we went. We rose smoothly to six feet or so from the ground, and spun around to hover-taxi to the runway area. John made this look so easy that I was already thinking, blimey this looks fun.

We taxied to an area of the airfield where there were no aircraft movements. He then demonstrated the amazing directional capabilities of a helicopter compared with fixed-wing flight. We zipped along sideways to the left, then to the right, at the same speed. We stopped, still hovering at about six feet off of the ground, then started to go backwards. This gave me such a buzz.

After showing me the flexibility of the helicopter when close to the ground, John called up for a departure, VFR for local navigation. We sped along the runway and gradually climbed up to what seemed to me fifty feet or thereabouts, then we veered quite sharply to the right, over the top of some large deciduous trees in full leaf, and descended again to about twenty feet.

We were now heading at quite a speed towards another row of trees in the distance. As we were getting closer, John gave the collective a yank with his right arm, giving the engine a full amount of beans, and at the same time pulling the nose of the helicopter up. We lifted at such rate of knots it was breath-taking. The beating of the rotor blades in the air frightened the wood pigeons out of the trees. They took off in a flutter in all directions, fearful of the huge, noisy bird flying towards them. We both laughed.

John said, 'I love doing that, it works every time.'

G ROLO then climbed westwards to a height of around 2000 feet. Once it was established in straight and level flight, John glanced at me to check I was ready to have a go myself.

'Now you can take over. Don't forget, you need only very small inputs to the controls to keep it straight and level.'

Flying Lima Oscar straight and level was not too difficult, as the controls react in a similar way to fixed-wing, but require a far lighter touch.

John took control again, and said, 'I'll show you the shortest runway you've ever seen.'

We started to descend, and soon were skimming over a very large field at an altitude of about thirty feet. I was scanning all around to see this runway, but couldn't see anything that resembled any runway I have ever landed on.

John kept grinning as he said, 'Have you seen it yet?'

I replied, 'No, not yet …' then did a double take, 'Unless it's what I think it might be …'

John laughed, and said, 'Yep, that's it.'

We slowed up, and gradually descended further, until we were hovering over a World War Two concrete pill box, not much more than twelve feet in diameter.

G ROLO very slowly, under the expert pilot skills of Mr Dines, descended and came to rest, sitting on top of the pill box with the rotors still spinning. It was a surreal experience, sitting inside a helicopter on top of the pill box, which was about ten feet tall. After a minute or two, John lifted the collective, and Lima Oscar effortlessly rose in to the air, racing away like an aerial superbike back in the direction of Redhill. As we got closer to the airfield, John called up the tower for re-join and landing instructions. In addition, he asked for an auto-rotation on finals. In essence this is the procedure for landing a helicopter when the engine has failed. It is not for the faint hearted.

We were just inside the airfield perimeter on final approach when John lowered the collective. I can best describe this as something like driving your car at sixty miles per hour, then pressing down on the clutch. The engine is no longer powering the wheels, and you slow down. But in a helicopter, it's a bit different. We were around 1800 feet above the airfield. G ROLO dropped like a stone. John was holding the cyclic stick back towards his knees, to keep the helicopter travelling straight and level at the same time as descending. It was the air rushing up through the rotors as we descended fast that saved us. When we were about fifty feet above ground, John pulled up the collective and the energy transferred from the rotors gave us about thirty seconds of lift. We touched down on both skids, and slid forward about fifty yards, no more. I could not believe what I had just experienced. Obviously, John was a highly skilled pilot, and maybe not all pilots have his experience, but it does give some comfort to think, if the unthinkable happens, there is a chance of survival in a helicopter.

The last element of my trial lesson was being given the chance to hover at around ten feet off of the ground.

John demonstrated this first, then said, 'Now you can try.'

He handed the controls to me when we were hovering solidly, as if we were back on that pill box. However, it couldn't have been more than thirty seconds after I had the controls, that Lima Oscar was rearing up, then lunging forward, like a bucking bronco in a Texan rodeo. I had a few more tries at this, every time with the same outcome.

We both laughed, and John steered us gracefully back to the apron where we had started my lesson, and gently landed G ROLO back on to that piece of Surrey concrete behind the control tower at Redhill Aerodrome.

We had a debrief back in his office, and John said that if I wanted to learn to fly helicopters, he would be pleased to teach me. I recounted my experience to my family, and friends alike, but decided I would not be adding rotary wing to my fixed-wing qualifications. My leisure time was limited by pressure of work, and I wanted to increase my fixed-wing experience.

7

Salutary Tales

'It's always better to be on the ground, wishing you were up in the air, than to be airborne but wishing you were on the ground.'

MARGARET BUTLER

Not Always Plain Sailing

Saturday 11th February 1995

I can't deny that sometimes I have made a decision I have later regretted, much like any other human being on this wonderful planet. Fortunately, there have not been too many, and so far, none that have resulted in injury. Let me explain.

By 1995 I had been flying for six years, and at times suffered with a condition I call 'Must Go Flying Now Syndrome'. It's a condition where the desire to go flying over rides the training you have received, and all the good advice imparted to you by more experienced pilots, your instructors and peers.

One Saturday in February I had decided to go flying alone. The weather was fine when I left East Farleigh, a bit grey with some cloud, but nothing to worry about. It took about three-quarters of an hour to drive to Biggin Hill from East Farleigh, so, on the journey I had plenty of time to anticipate my forthcoming flight.

At Biggin, I was given the keys to G BPWS, one of the King Air Cessna 172 fleet. The weather had deteriorated by now. It was getting quite windy, and there was light drizzle too. In these conditions, I should have seriously considered: 'Is this flight really necessary?' to which the obvious answer is, 'No!'

However, I was experiencing a severe attack of 'Must Go Flying Now Syndrome' and seemed to have put my training and experience of the past six years inside my flight bag, and left it there. I remember walking out of the club house, and along the path to the apron, where the fleet was parked, looking up at the weather and thinking: 'That's not too bad, I'll be fine. I have an IMC rating, I am invincible.'

Invincible is the word that should never enter a pilot's vocabulary. I must have been in denial, with an overwhelming urge to get airborne. I continued to complete the pre-flight checks, climbed inside Whiskey Sierra and started the engine, still not taking a full account of the prevailing winds and rapidly deteriorating weather conditions.

It takes between five and seven minutes to taxi to the hold for runway 21, which was in use that day, and still I had not really appreciated the worsening weather. I just wanted to get in the air, and in total control of G BPWS.

The ATC on shift that Saturday morning gave me clearance to take off and the wind speed and direction, which I think went straight over my head.

We sped along the runway. The strengthening wind pushed Whiskey Sierra into the cold air with great force. I remember passing through 500 feet at the far end of runway 21, when cloud swallowed me and Whiskey Sierra instantly.

Now that was the point where, if the same thing was to happen today, I would take the power off immediately, so we could descend out of the cloud as quickly as we had gone into it. I would call the tower, tell them I was going to make a low-level circuit, keeping sight of the ground, and immediately return to land on runway 21, to end the detail for the day.

I am sure you have guessed that was not what happened. Instead, I kept on climbing, now flying on instruments, intent on gaining height, as height is safety. I enjoy flying on instruments, and can do it accurately, keeping the wings straight and level. But the weather was worsening all the time. I was unaware how strong the wind had become, now I was airborne and in thick cloud.

As I recall, it felt like forever, flying on instruments, alone in thick cloud. Fortunately, my concentration didn't waiver and I did remember a piece of advice from Margaret.

'Whatever is happening with the aircraft, keep flying as you would normally until you can't fly it any longer. Don't panic, just concentrate on the flying.'

With those words uppermost in my mind, I kept my head space clear, and kept scanning the instruments. All of a sudden, light filled the aircraft. I had broken out of the cloud into an area of open sky, and to my surprise, I was over the Dartford Crossing at around 2000 feet.

This gave me a bit of breathing space to look around, gather my thoughts and slow my mind down. I then assessed my options, which were few. I decided to attempt an instrument landing system (ILS) approach back to Biggin Hill.

So, having made this decision, I contacted Thames Radar and requested vectors onto the ILS at Biggin. I put in the ILS frequency, and was vectored to intercept it and start my approach completely blind. The cloud was opaque and mid-grey, totally obscuring everything outside the aeroplane.

By now, the scan of the instruments was getting ever quicker, and the two black lines on the VOR instrument started to move. My aim when making an ILS approach is to keep the lines perfectly crossed in the centre of the dial, with one passing from the 9 to the 3 positions, indicating the glide slope. The other line has to be kept dead centre in the 12 to the 6 positions; this confirms the correct glide path.

Unfortunately, the weather was so bad, and the wind was really gusting, that the two needles seemed to have a mind of their own. As soon as they crossed each other, they just passed, dancing all over the face of the dial.

Suddenly, I was below the cloud and realised I was getting too low, so abandoned this ILS approach. As I have said, height is safety. I initiated a climb back up to around 2000 feet, and again found, more by luck than judgement, some cloudless air space. I repeated this procedure one more time, but sadly with the same outcome.

Again, I found myself over the Thames, near Dartford. At about 1500 feet above sea level, I was flying just below the cloud base and thankfully was able to see the river below.

It was at this point that I received a call on the radio from Thames Radar. They informed me that the King Air chief flying instructor on shift that day had phoned the Biggin Hill control tower to see if I had called up to return. Biggin ATC relayed this enquiry to Thames Radar and were told that I was trying to make an ILS approach, but was not having much success.

King Air then phoned Thames Radar and asked them to talk to me, to find out whether I could divert to Southend Airport using visual flight rules. I replied that I believed I could, so I started to fly eastwards along the Thames, losing height all the time, as the cloud base was lowering fast. Thames Radar also said that it was no surprise my attempts at an ILS approach to Biggin Hill Airport was unsuccessful, as the wind in that area was gusting to fifty knots.

By the time I had reached Canvey Island, with only a few miles to go to Southend Airport, it was raining quite hard, but I just concentrated on flying the plane. I called up Southend ATC and was given clearance to land on runway 23. By the time I was turning on to final approach, the cloud base was down to five hundred feet or so, and seemed to be pushing me down, lower and lower, as I was making my approach, with the rain getting heavier by the minute.

I crossed over the public road, just off the edge of runway 23, took more power off, and with huge relief felt the smooth tarmac of the Southend Airport runway beneath the rolling wheels of Whiskey Sierra. I left the runway at the far end, turned left and taxied to the apron outside the control tower. I parked next to a medium-sized passenger jet, an Airbus A320.

I climbed out of Whiskey Sierra. The rain was almost horizontal. I dashed to the entrance door to the tower, briefly looking back at G BPWS battered by this downpour, as heavy and relentless as an Indian monsoon. I realised how lucky I had been to survive this flight with both the plane and me intact, and to be standing on the ground in Essex. In normal conditions, the flight from Biggin to Southend would take around twenty minutes. On that day, I took off at 09:20 and landed at 10:35.

I reported to the reception in the control tower, and paid my landing fee. Then I phoned King Air, and told them that their plane and its pilot were safely on the ground at Southend Airport.

I was informed that normal procedure in this instance was for me to make my own way home. At my expense, an instructor would travel by taxi to Southend, assess the situation and fly the plane back to Biggin whenever he deemed it safe to do so.

Having no option, I agreed to this and decided to wait for the instructor to arrive. He turned up just after midday, and I recounted the whole story to him.

He didn't criticise me, but said, 'You'll never make that mistake again.'

I agreed with him. I hadn't met this instructor before. Like Islam, with whom I'd flown the Seneca III, he was a first officer with a commercial airline, so had a full IR rating. He suggested an alternative solution for my return to Kent. Rather than me making my way home by train, since the weather was starting to improve somewhat, he suggested that I fly with him back to Biggin.

I thought, 'If he's happy to fly in these weather conditions, so am I.' Immediately I replied, 'Yes, I'd love to.'

We took off from Southend at 12:55, and landed back at Biggin at 13:40. I flew the plane, and he took care of the radio. If we had run into more trouble, having an IR rated pilot in the adjacent seat would have made a considerable difference.

Although it was a bumpy ride back, I loved every second of the flight. I did have to pay for the instructor's taxi to Southend, and for his time on our return flight. However, I think the lesson that I learnt from that day was worth every penny. Needless to say, I have never made the same mistake again.

The Darker Side

You've probably realised by now that I seriously enjoy flying. Whether I'm taking a plane for a local flight alone, or going with a friend on a jolly to France, or taking someone for their first flight in a light aircraft, enjoyment is fundamental. Part of the pleasure comes from knowing that I have done everything I can to ensure a safe flight.

I can't see the point of pursuing a hobby unless it brings pleasure, fulfilment and fun. In large part, the fun of flying comes from becoming an ever-better pilot by building hours, flying different plane types, visiting new airfields and refreshing my knowledge and technical skills.

There is a serious side to aviation, and especially light aviation. As long as you have enough money to pay for the lessons and if you have been able to pass a driving test to use the public roads, providing you can also pass the medical and are willing to do a bit of studying, then you could probably get a private pilot's licence. However, holding that PPL could have far-reaching consequences, for you and other people.

During the thirty-one years that I have held my PPL, I have known several people who have lost their lives whilst flying light aircraft. I have also seen video footage and read accounts of the deaths of private pilots, killed whilst flying. In nearly every case, the disaster was due entirely or mostly, to pilot error. Fatal crashes are rarely caused by mechanical or structural failure of the aeroplane.

We PPLs have a serious responsibility not only to our passengers, but also to people on the ground and their property. As I have mentioned already, I have never, ever, drunk any alcohol before flying, or during a day trip when I have been the pilot in command. I wouldn't jeopardise my licence and my life, nor the lives of my passengers, for the sake of a glass of wine.

I have been to Le Touquet on several occasions, and have seen another pilot fly in from the UK in command of a Cessna or Piper, lock up his plane and walk to the airport restaurant and order a beer. Later in the day I have been in Le Touquet town and spotted the same pilot in a restaurant drinking wine with his lunch. It may have been just one or two drinks, but the flying regulations make it clear that alcohol and aviation must not be mixed. Taking control of an aircraft after alcohol has been consumed is forbidden.

I am sure most people would expect all pilots to comply with the regulations and would be horrified at the thought that any pilot could be so reckless as drink and fly. But the truth is, not all pilots appear to accept that the rules also apply to them.

Some years ago, when I used to buy *Pilot*, and *Flyer*, I read an article in one or other publication that gave an account of a fatal incident. A plane had been observed flying erratically. It was spotted flying at low altitude over towns and roads. Eventually the PPL at the controls of the plane crashed it, killing himself, but fortunately no one else. When the emergency services got to the site of the crash, they found an almost empty bottle of whisky in the wreckage; the post-mortem revealed that the pilot had consumed a large quantity of alcohol.

Another incident about which I read took place at Bournemouth Airport. A student PPL was building up solo hours, in accordance with the syllabus. To the horror of the instructor watching him from the ground, the student had completed a circuit, and was approaching the airfield to continue. He landed on the runway, retracted one stage of flap, so that he had the flaps set for take-off, and proceeded to climb away again for another circuit. He climbed to around 500 feet, then nose-dived straight into a field and was killed instantly. A verdict of suicide was recorded.

Bad decisions can be so much more serious when flying, compared with driving a car, and can have far-reaching consequences, which is why, as anyone who has flown with me knows, I will never hesitate to cancel a flight if I am not totally satisfied that the weather is suitable for a safe flight. If I have the slightest doubt about the airworthiness of the plane that I am about to fly I will not take-off. Although I did fly a Robin with a problem, which I will flesh out in another chapter.

I used to have a client who also held a PPL, which I had not realised had lapsed. He was not a particular favourite of mine. That's an understatement really; he was arrogant, and within his company he had the reputation of being a bully, but I had to deal with him when chasing for the payment of our invoices.

My client was flying to Le Touquet with another, considerably younger guy who owned his own aeroplane. The younger PPL didn't have an IMC rating, and my client who had held an IMC rating at one time had let it lapse. I learnt later that he hadn't flown as pilot in command for more than a year.

They left Le Touquet with the owner of the plane in the right-hand seat, not the captain's seat where he should have been, as the only current PPL holder on board.

The weather on the way back to Biggin Hill deteriorated rapidly. The correct decision would have been to turn around and head for Lydd, landing there to wait on the ground until the weather improved. I can imagine, however, if my client was sitting in the captain's seat, he would probably have bullied the younger man. They called the Biggin Hill tower and said they were going to make an ILS approach. At this point he made the classic error. The altimeter pressure setting was not changed from QNH, the height above sea level to QFE, the height above the destination airfield level.

The plane flew at speed straight into the ground, a few miles before they reached the airport. Both men were killed. The altimeter would have told them that they still had around 500 feet of height, but Biggin Hill is around 500 feet above sea level.

Sadly, experience does not always guarantee the safe conclusion to a flight. Sometimes, well-respected pilots with thousands of hours of flying experience can become complacent, or fly when tired, or lose concentration, with disastrous consequences.

David, an acquaintance of mine for twenty years, was killed alongside another hugely experienced pilot in January 2019. Whilst bringing an aircraft from Portugal back to Britain they flew into the side of a mountain in the south of France. If I was to put money on the last person who would be involved in a fatal collision, caused by making a fundamental error, it would have been him.

David was not only a private pilot, but also an instructor and a qualified M3 aircraft engineer. He owned a Cessna, among other aircraft. He made his living variously from maintaining other people's aircraft, banner towing and instructing or doing check-outs for other PPLs.

I won't go in to the detail of what happened in France and why, but when I heard of David's death, I was shocked and couldn't believe it. Everyone I spoke to at Rochester who had also known David agreed that if it could happen to him, it could happen to anyone.

It was a wake-up call to take nothing for granted, to re-double my concentration and to check and re-check every instrument setting whilst flying.

I have never been embarrassed about being cautious. If I don't feel happy about something before take-off, I won't hesitate to cancel the flight.

Elly once said to me, 'You are right to be cautious whenever you fly, Les. There are old pilots, and there are bold pilots, but very few old, bold pilots.' Her words are always in the back of my mind when I go flying.

Civil Aviation Authority safety evenings are periodically held at Biggin Hill Airport and Rochester Airport. I try to attend them whenever I can. These events are provided free of charge, and make a valuable contribution to aviation safety. Sad to say, I have seen many videos of incidents in which bad decisions made by light aircraft pilots have led inevitably to crashes and fatalities.

* * *

On a lighter note, I once offered to fly G BOGI, the Robin DR 400 I used to fly regularly, to Redhill Aerodrome, for some maintenance by an aviation engineer called Al. He had moved his business from Rochester to Redhill. G BOGI was running in the red zone on the oil temperature gauge during flight, and in a sort of Catch-22 situation, no other pilot, even the owner, would fly G BOGI to Redhill to get the problem fixed. I heard about this, and offered my services. This meant I got free flying time. On my way to Rochester, the owner Alan phoned me whilst I was driving along the M20.

He said, 'Les, thanks for taking GI to Redhill. If it overheats and the engine seizes, you have my permission to land in a field. Good luck.'

I didn't say this to him, but thought, 'If the engine stops, never mind his permission, I'm going to do whatever it takes to save my life and hope it doesn't damage the plane too much in the process.'

I remember that several people based at Rochester had heard on the grapevine that I was going to fly G BOGI to Redhill, and they all wished me luck.

Even Kelvin, in the control tower looked me in the eye and said, 'Good luck.'

He then shook my hand. It felt as if I was going to test fly the latest concept aircraft from NASA.

Being aware of the problem of the engine oil overheating, I took off and climbed to around 2000 feet, where I throttled back to around 2100 rpm, to just maintain height, keeping a very close eye on the gauge. When the needle just nudged the red zone, I retarded the throttle some more, which had a slight effect on the needle; I now could just see a small gap between the red zone, and the normal operating zone, and we were only losing around 50 feet a minute. I nursed the two of us to Redhill and landed on the northerly grass runway, then taxied to Al's hangar. The problem was soon resolved, and I flew G BOGI back to Rochester, arriving at around 18:00. I had enjoyed the flight, despite all the disquieting comments prior to my departure, and it hadn't cost me anything.

* * *

I have deliberately included my salutary tales at this point, because I don't want to end my memoir leaving you with the impression that flying is risky and frightening. Flying light aircraft is a wonderful hobby, with a good safety record, and fewer annual fatalities than golf, I am reliably informed. So, if you ever get the chance to take a flight or a trial lesson, grasp it with both hands, I promise that you won't forget it, and who knows, you may even enjoy it.

Beware, Greedy Passenger!

During the summer months of 1994, I continued to fly three different aircraft types: the twin-engine GA 7 Cougar, several Cessna 172s, and also added the Grumman American AA5 B Tiger to my log book.

Flying the Tiger was noticeably different from other aircraft I had flown. Although it had a low wing like the Piper PA 28 Cadet, that's where the similarity ended. First of all, it was much easier to handle on the ground due to the nose wheel being the castoring type. The Piper and Cessna have only limited movement, left and right, on their nose wheel, so when you are trying to move the plane whilst it is on the apron, it takes quite a bit of physical strength. However, the AA5 B Tiger is relatively effortless to move on the ground. If you want to turn the plane around you just need to gently push on the leading edge, at the end of the wing, and the castoring nose wheel will spin, much like the wheels on a supermarket trolley. And around the plane goes.

The downside to the castoring nose wheel is that you have to really take care when you land. You must not touch down on the nose wheel first. Not at all, not even a little. If you land nose wheel first in a Tiger it could collapse, throwing the propellor into the ground, and potentially breaking the engine in the process. Nose wheel landing could result in huge and costly damage. I found landing on the two main wheels first relatively easy and didn't get fooled into bouncing on the nose wheel when landing, if the approach speed was a little high.

Margaret and Elly both taught me that if the speed is a little high, just keep the nose up, and let the speed bleed off the wings, so the two main wheels touch the ground before the nose wheel. Keep it in the air.

The Tiger certainly lived up to its name. I used to fly an AA5 B from Biggin Hill, with the call sign G TYGA. Surely, that cannot have been a coincidence, any more than the call sign G KDET on the Piper Cadet I flew sometimes?

On the take-off roll, the Tiger had an attitude as it built up speed very quickly. Once in the air, it did not disappoint either. The control yoke on the Tiger is quite a bit smaller than those of similar light aircraft, which also helps give it the feel of something very sporty. Much as a car with a smaller steering wheel feels sporty.

When I was seventeen, my first car was a 105 E Ford Anglia. The original Ford steering wheel was huge, but as soon as I had bought and fitted a ten-inch diameter leather-bound steering wheel, the feeling was so different, quite sporty.

The Tiger reacts very quickly when banking, which is especially exhilarating when carrying out steep, sixty-degree angle-of-bank turns. In the cruise, the Tiger managed a very respectable 125 to 130 knots indicated air speed. The flight to Shoreham Airport, just west of Brighton, took around forty minutes. I regret that I don't know of any AA5 B Tigers that are available locally to hire and fly nowadays, or I would be flying one.

We visited Shoreham one Sunday in May 1994. Jean and I were sitting outside the restaurant, just by the apron, where Golf Alpha was parked. We had left from Biggin to fly to Shoreham for tea and buns. As we enjoyed our afternoon tea another AA5 B flew in.

It looked almost brand new, was finished in polar white, and on both sides it had a graphic of a tiger that stretched from the propellor to the tail of the plane. It was more than eye-catching with its black and orange markings, sitting on the parking area. I must confess to being envious of the owner of such a striking-looking aeroplane.

The Tiger wasn't the only new type I flew in 1994, I also had a check-out in a different type of Cessna 172. This one was called a Reims Rocket!

G AWCN was built in 1968 and had a variable pitch propellor, like the twin-engine GA7 Cougar. This, combined with an engine with lots of grunt, made it a safe and stable aircraft to use when flying with four adults up.

Now, about the greedy passenger. At this time, we lived in the village of East Farleigh, about three miles south-west of Maidstone. Living in the same lane was a client of mine. I had realised early on that being able to fly a light aircraft could give me a unique platform for entertaining clients. I had invited my client, a director of an engineering company, and his wife to join Jean and me for lunch in France, one Sunday in August 1994. Dieppe was our destination. Back in the nineties there were few companies that offered such unusual personal entertaining. My client, of course, jumped at the invitation.

They lived about a hundred yards along the road from us, so we collected them from their home and drove together to Biggin Hill. On arrival, I filed our flight plan with ATC, then led my party through customs. I carried out the pre-flight checks on Charlie November on the apron outside the control tower. With maximum take-off pitch selected, and full power from the engine, the four of us were soon roaring along runway 21. We headed south, coasting out over Lydd Airport, flying directly to Boulogne, then followed the French coast until we turned inland to Dieppe.

It took around an hour and twenty minutes to get there, and I remember it was a very stable and smooth flight. On this occasion the Dieppe douane was open, unlike my previous visit in the Cougar which had coincided with a French public holiday.

Once the aircraft had been shut down and locked, and we had cleared customs and passport control, the four of us got into a taxi and headed straight to the centre of Dieppe. I soon found a respectable-looking French restaurant and we went in.

The maître d' welcomed us and enquired, 'Une table pour quatre, monsieur?'

We were soon seated and browsing the menu. When entertaining, it was my habit to invite clients to choose the wine and whatever they would like from the menu.

Now this is where the story really starts. My client chose Kir Royale for himself and his wife as an aperitif. Jean and I had lemonade. During my thirty-one years as a private pilot, I have never, and I mean never, had an alcoholic drink at any time during a day when I have planned to fly.

My client necked his aperitif, and ordered another. I just took a mental note. We ordered our meals. I stuck to a simple poulet et pommes frites for my entrée. He ordered a huge plat des fruits de mer for his starter, then a rich, meaty entrée, followed by a creamy dessert. I declined dessert.

All of this food he washed down with at least a bottle and a half of good French red wine, and to finish off his luncheon he ordered a couple of large measures of cognac. We must have been in the restaurant for nearly three hours.

Eventually we left the restaurant and decided to wander through Dieppe. Sight-seeing is one of the many pleasures of visiting this delightful Normandy town, with its pastel stucco and timber-framed buildings. Houses are adorned with window boxes, exploding with colour from the red, pink and white geraniums that you only see in France. My client started to complain of feeling unwell.

When I asked him, 'In what way are you feeling unwell?'

'I think I'm going to be sick ...' With that, he ran into a little alleyway between two shops, and I heard a horrendous retching sound echoing back down the alley.

I thought but didn't say, 'This is no surprise. You couldn't stuff all that rich food in your mouth quickly enough ... and mixed with all the alcohol you've necked this was bound to happen. Thanks for spoiling the day for the rest of us.'

I felt sorry for his wife, who was very embarrassed. Slowly, we continued our walk through the town, but he disappeared again to vomit a couple more times.

He then said, 'I'm afraid I can't stay any longer, I feel so bad.'

I maintained my demeanour as host and said, albeit through gritted teeth, 'No problem, I'll call a taxi to take us back to the airfield.'

The drive back to the airfield seemed to take forever. We were all afraid he would disgrace us by throwing up in the French taxi. The moment we arrived back at Dieppe Airport he went straight to the men's toilet, announcing he now had diarrhoea.

I started to carry out my pre-flight checks on Charlie November, and then filed my flight plan, for our return journey to Biggin. After a while, he staggered out to the aircraft, looking dishevelled and pale. He climbed into the passenger seat beside me. Before I had started the engine, he opened the door again to rush back to the sanctuary of the toilet. We sat there patiently waiting for him to re-emerge. His wife was extremely cross with him by now. I felt like leaving him there for being so bloody greedy. Because he wasn't paying, he had gorged himself almost to oblivion. Eventually, he returned to Charlie November, climbed into his seat and fastened the seat belt.

'Right,' I thought, 'Let's get home.'

I turned the key in the ignition. To my utter disbelief, there was no response; nothing but silence. I tried another couple of times, still nothing. What more could go wrong? We all climbed out of the plane. The others waited whilst I walked back to the bar, where the manager, who was also the ATC, was at the end of his shift and waiting for us to depart. He was enjoying his **Gauloises** and a glass of Cognac in the company of a young woman. I told him about the farcical situation in which I now found myself, and asked whether he had any helpful suggestions.

He shrugged, smiled and said, 'Go back to your plane, I'll be right over.'

A minute or two later, he drove over to the plane in an old Citroen. He pulled up close to G AWCN, got out of the car, and instructed his girlfriend to sit in the driver's seat. He retrieved some jump leads from the boot of his car, then leaned into the Reims Rocket, and pulled away the panel on the back seat, exposing the battery.

He said, 'It's probably flat.'

He attached the jump leads to the battery, then attached the other ends to his car battery. We climbed back into Charlie November. He called to his girlfriend, telling her to rev the engine. The old Citroen was coughing and spluttering like a fifty-a-day smoker.

The manager ATC said to me, 'Try the engine, mon ami.'

I turned the key, and to my relief, the engine burst into life. He unclipped the jump leads and stood on the grass beside the plane.

He said, 'You have permission to take off, monsieur. Au revoir. Safe journey. Bon voyage.'

I thanked him. Without further ado, I taxied to the hold of runway 31. With full power we sped off and climbed up to 3000 feet. We were flying towards a sea fog, which I could see in the distance.

During our direct flight back across about sixty miles of Channel, I glanced at my client, who was sitting there, eyes closed, trying not to breathe or make any sudden movements, in case his bowels didn't hold.

I told him, 'If you feel you need the toilet, don't let me know, because I will have no choice but to push you out of the plane over the sea.'

Obviously, it was said in jest, but inwardly I was deadly serious.

We had no further electrical troubles with G AWCN during the flight. We landed back at Biggin Hill around 18:20, where we cleared customs with the bottles of wine my client bought for himself. The drive back to East Farleigh was very quiet. I was relieved to see the back of our neighbours that day.

8

New Horizons

'Flying is the second greatest thrill known to man; landing is the first.'

Bembridge and Britannia

Wednesday, 23rd November 1994

In the early autumn of 1994, I found a new destination for lunch and business entertaining: the airfield at Bembridge, on the Isle of Wight. Although only five miles from Sandown Airport, Bembridge Airport was popular with PPLs and I soon discovered why. It has a nice concrete runway, 837 metres in length, orientated 12/30 and a friendly, helpful ATC.

I visited Bembridge for the first time on 5th October 1994. I had been recommended to visit a pub and restaurant named the Crab and Lobster, perched on top of the cliffs at Bembridge. I took Stan along too, so we could check out the restaurant. It proved to be a very good pub, and was only about a fifteen-minute taxi ride from Bembridge airfield.

Whilst sitting at a table in the restaurant, you had a wonderful view of the Solent, towards Hayling Island. So, with the Crab and Lobster having passed our quality control test, it was added to my list of destinations where I could entertain clients, as well as family and friends.

The first clients I took to Bembridge were two guys from an air conditioning company: Brian Hopwood, who was the owner, and his colleague, Mick Wincott.

On approach to Bembridge, when we were about five miles away, I called up the tower to request joining and landing information. After the usual exchanges with ATC, I asked them to book a taxi, so that it would be waiting for me at the control tower car park to take my guests and me to the Crab and Lobster. ATC were always pleased to help; they were earning income from the landing fee; the local taxi firms were being used; and eventually the pub landlord would relieve me of a significant sum of money. So, it was a win-win all around.

The Crab and Lobster was a popular pub, so before we took off that morning, I had telephoned and booked a table for the three of us, next to the window overlooking the Solent. We sat down and ordered our meals, enjoying the marvellous sea view from our high vantage point on the cliffs. Then the landlord walked over and pointed to an elegant three-masted and one-funnel ship steaming through the Solent.

He said, 'There goes the Royal Yacht Britannia. We frequently see her leaving Portsmouth, though not for much longer, sadly.'

Not being one to miss an opportunity, I said to my clients, 'If you listen carefully, you should be able to hear the band of the Royal Marines on the stern deck. I've arranged for them to play whilst we are having lunch, as they are passing Bembridge.'

Brian and Mick looked at each other incredulously, then at me and the landlord. The penny dropped and we all laughed. The day was going well. After a convivial lunch, the taxi was recalled to convey us back to the airfield for our return to Biggin Hill.

The return flight provided the opportunity to show my clients some magnificent coastline, rolling countryside and familiar landmarks as we overflew Hampshire, Sussex and Kent. Chichester Harbour, Goodwood Racecourse, Shoreham Airport, the Seven Sisters cliffs near Beachy Head; then turning north, heading inland we flew over Bewl Water, Scotney Castle, Tunbridge Wells, Sevenoaks and back to Biggin.

Over the next few years, I returned to Bembridge several times, flying there in different aircraft types, but I never again saw *HMY Britannia* in the Solent.

Endnote

Her Majesty's Yacht Britannia, more often called the *Royal Yacht Britannia*, is the former royal yacht of Queen Elizabeth II.

Britannia was built in John Brown's shipyard on Clydebank in Scotland. She was launched by Queen Elizabeth II on 16th April 1953, commissioned on 11th January 1954 and sailed on her maiden voyage from Portsmouth to Malta in April 1954.

During her forty-three years in service as the royal yacht, *Britannia* travelled more than a million nautical miles and made nearly a thousand visits to foreign destinations and in British waters.

Britannia underwent a major refit in 1987. The Ministry of Defence anticipated she would need a further refit in 1997, costing some £17 million, but this would only prolong her life for a further five years. In view of her age, even after the refit she would be difficult to maintain and expensive to run. In 1994 the government of the day decided this expenditure could not be justified, so decided to decommission *Britannia* in 1997.

The royal yacht's final foreign mission was to convey the last governor of Hong Kong, Sir Chris Patten, and the Prince of Wales back from Hong Kong after its handover to the People's Republic of China on 1st July 1997.

Not-So-High Over Hong Kong

Chinese New Year 1997

In the nineties, in addition to our main business, Stan and I had an engineering company, manufacturing and installing weather and acoustic louvres, silencers, and other engineering products fabricated from metal.

I can't really remember how we got the enquiry for the manufacture and supply of acoustic louvres for two railway stations in Hong Kong. One station was on the island, and the other was at the race track at Sha Tin, in the New Territories. As I had already been to Hong Kong in 1987 and had some business contacts there, I decided to visit the sites, to inspect our products which were being installed by local contractors.

I flew from Stansted Airport one Friday afternoon after a week at work. My route was from Stansted to Schiphol Airport, south-west of Amsterdam in the Netherlands. There I transferred to a KLM Jumbo for the non-stop flight to Hong Kong.

It was a real march from the arrival terminal at Schiphol, where my plane landed, to the departure terminal where my continuing flight was to leave. At times I felt myself breaking into a trot to make sure I didn't miss the connection.

At the departure desk for the KLM flight, I discovered that I had been allocated a seat at the rear of the plane where smoking was permitted. It's hard to believe now that smoking was permitted on aircraft, and passengers would light up their cigarettes with lighters, or even matches. Thank goodness things have changed so much for the better. I loathe the habit, so asked if I could be transferred to a non-smoking seat. To my surprise and delight the lady behind the desk consulted her lists.

'I can put you in a non-smoking seat in first class. Would that be acceptable?' she enquired.

An upgrade at no extra cost. That has never happened to me again.

'Thank you' I replied, relieved because it had been a long week.

The flight from Amsterdam to Kai Tak Airport in Hong Kong was sublime, relaxing back in that huge first-class seat, with only one other passenger sitting next to me. Plenty of leg room, a glass of champagne as we were preparing for departure, followed by a delicious three-course meal.

Later, an attentive cabin steward proffered a cosy blanket and a pouch of complimentary toiletries. The lights were dimmed in the cabin.

As I fell asleep, I thought, 'How the other half live.'

We landed at Kai Tak Airport, in the heart of Hong Kong, early on Sunday morning. Once I'd cleared customs and immigration, I found a taxi and went straight to the Furama Hotel. I had stayed there once before, when Stan and I visited in 1988. It's near the waterfront, just a five-minute walk from the Star Ferry that has crossed Victoria Harbour from Hong Kong Island to Kowloon-side for the past 120 years, and is Hong Kong's oldest form of public transport.

After getting some sleep, I made arrangements to visit both sites during the next couple of days. I was gratified to see our products, manufactured in our factory in West Kingsdown, installed on either side of the railway track in Hong Kong.

The noise of trains entering and leaving the stations had been disturbing residents living in the apartment blocks close to the track. Until I saw the acoustic louvres installed, I hadn't appreciated just how close to the track people were living in the densely populated residential districts. I noticed there were small areas of tarmac between the buildings, where groups of boys were energetically playing basketball, shooting into a hoop mounted on the facade of the block where they lived. I discovered that I had arrived towards the end of the Chinese New Year holiday, which explained why they weren't at school.

I was in Hong Kong for about six days. After visiting both sites and making a report back to my colleagues in the UK, I contacted another client in Hong Kong. The last time I had seen Achim Muelbert was in his office in Tai Pei, the capital of Taiwan. We had completed another acoustic engineering project, in Kaohsiung, a port city in the south of the island. Achim had been transferred to another office, this time on the island of Hong Kong. I visited Stanley Market to buy flowers, and then spent an enjoyable evening with Achim and his wife, Eleanore.

With a day left to amuse myself in Hong Kong, I wondered whether there might be a chance of hiring a Cessna or Piper to fly over the local area. I had brought my log book and PPL just in case.

In those days, we had to resort to the Yellow Pages directory to find suppliers of products or services. Every hotel room had a copy. I found an airfield with a flying club offering PPL hire at a place called Shek Kong, a small town in the New Territories. Public transport is excellent in Hong

Kong, so I could get there easily enough. A couple of phone calls and it was arranged.

The next morning, I took a train as far as I could, then a taxi from the station to the airfield. The ride was an experience in itself, along rural roads through the countryside, past small houses made from block work and corrugated sheet. A scatter of people wearing traditional conical straw hats were working in the fields, picking vegetables. A barking dog chased the taxi.

This airfield had been RAF Sek Kong. It had a good long runway, the usual cluster of buildings and hangars, a few aircraft parked on the grass and a control tower. I went into the club reception, introduced myself, and presented my PPL and log book. Instead of having a check-out in the plane and then flying alone, I decided to hire an instructor to fly with me and be my guide. I am afraid I can't remember his name, but I do remember he was a Kiwi, a cheerful New Zealander, in his mid-twenties and he was building experience as an instructor before moving on eventually to fly commercial aircraft.

After the formalities were out of the way, he showed me to the apron, and pointed to a Cessna 172 with the call sign VR HRH. I checked out Romeo Hotel, as I had done with so many 172s in England, and soon we were on our way, gathering speed along the runway.

After take-off, we had to continue with a climbing turn, until we reached around 2000 feet, in order to fly away and clear the peaks that surrounded the airfield. The location of RAF Sek Kong was determined by topography, sited on the only large area of flat ground which is not marshy, behind the mountains that are the backdrop to Kowloon.

I continued to fly south-west towards Lantau Island, and reduced height to around 1500 feet. My instructor pointed out the massive reclamation project below, and the building site that was to become Chek Lap Kok, Hong Kong's new international airport. It is one of the largest and most advanced in the world. Designed by Foster and Partners, it opened in 1998 replacing Kai Tak, which was then developed as a cruise ship port.

The next landmark to come into view was the enormous bronze Tian Tian Buddha, perched on a peak near the Po Lin monastery. The statue looks as if it has been sitting there for centuries, magnificent, with a serene expression; one hand vertical, and the other outstretched with the palm flat. Surprisingly it was only four years old then, having been completed in 1993.

From there we headed off in the direction of Hong Kong Island, and called up Kai Tak approach to inform them of our intentions, which were to fly into their traffic zone, as far as the airport. We would then turn and track back, crossing close to Kowloon-side, and make a return flight to Sek Kong.

Kai Tak replied and gave us permission for this route, and instructed me to remain below 500 feet at all times. Yes, below 500 feet at all times. This was music to my ears.

Immediately I put Romeo Hotel into a descent and flew at 500 feet over Silver Mine Bay, on the edge of the island, then out over the South China sea, at around 400 feet above the azure blue water below. This was the stuff of dreams.

We flew over ships anchored out to sea in the deeper water, because they were too large to moor up, transferring their cargoes on to smaller ships and junks. The smaller vessels then carried the goods into the many ports along the coastline of Kowloon. I noticed some crew, on the deck of a large ship, looking up and waving to us. I gave the wings a waggle to acknowledge their greeting.

Still at 400 feet, we flew along the edge of Hong Kong Island, and were level with the windows of high-rise apartments and office buildings. On we flew towards the runway at Kai Tak. Just before we reached the runway, my instructor told me to make a steep 180-degree turn, as we were a bit too close. Holy Moly! That was such a buzz, applying more power and pulling the controls back, to complete a tight turn for the return track, looking down at the buildings on Kowloon-side and the vehicles crawling along the roads below. This was turning out to be an incomparable flight.

Once we were away from Kowloon, climbing back up to 2000 feet, we headed for the New Territories. I cleared the mountains, and could see the airfield and runway in the distance. During the latter part of the return flight, I had been a little tardy in losing height, inevitably ending up quite high on final approach. I told the instructor that I still had too much height, so had decided to use the final stage of flap, which was forty degrees on this old Cessna.

With forty degrees of flaps engaged, the angle of approach you can achieve and still be at the correct landing speed is quite astonishing. It seems as if you are looking vertically down at the ground. I flared the 172 over the numbers, and it just kept floating. The instructor commented with a chuckle, 'The ground must be down there somewhere.'

We floated on ... and on ... and on ... then gently touched down on the main wheels, followed a moment later by the nose wheel.

After taxiing back to the apron, and shutting VR HRH down, I went into the office and paid, which to date, has been one of the best £250 I have ever spent. How many other people can put their name to such an experience?

Endnote

On 1st July 1997, Hong Kong, which had been a Crown Colony for more than a century, was peaceably handed back to China in a ceremony attended by numerous Chinese, British, and international dignitaries.

As soon as the handover ceremonies were completed, *HMY Britannia*, on her final foreign mission, sailed out of Hong Kong Harbour, with the Prince of Wales and the last governor of Hong Kong, Sir Chris Patten, on board. It was the end of an era.

You Can Rely on the RAF

Tuesday, 26th August 1997

In August 1997, I had a chat with Kelvin Carr, a friend of mine and manager of Rochester Airport. He recommended an airfield I had never visited before, Earls Colne (EGSR) near Colchester in Essex. Rural is the word that comes to mind when describing the location of the airfield, south-west of the village of the same name.

Earls Colne is one of twenty-seven historic military airfields in Essex dating from World War Two. Many more had been planned in the county, to accommodate US bomber groups. Flying Fortresses of the US Army Air Force's 94th Bomb Group arrived at Earls Colne in May 1943. The additional airfields planned were not required because the USA diverted some of its fleet and operations to North Africa.

Now, Earls Colne is a general aviation (GA) airfield. I was told by Kelvin that it is a lovely airfield to visit, and is right next to a golf course. I took off from Rochester at 17:00 hours on the 26th August, and flew over the Thames Estuary, keeping west of Southend Airport, and onwards over the Blackwater Estuary. Earls Colne is to the west of Colchester. Remembering Kelvin's words, when I could see Colchester away to the east on the tip of the starboard wing, I began looking out for a golf course. I assessed I was in the right area. From around 1500 feet, all the ground below me was green pasture, arable crops, and golf courses. There seemed to be dozens of golf courses. If you lived in that part of Essex, you could probably walk to a golf course in whichever town or village you happen to reside.

The lack of discernible features did not help me in my quest to find Earls Colne, which, by the way, does not have radio navigation aids. So doggedly I kept flying at 110 knots, whilst keeping a note of the time I had been flying. I should be able to see Earls Colne, but however hard I stared, nothing resembling an airfield stood out from the lush countryside below.

After another five minutes or so, in the distance, I could see a very long concrete runway. It seemed very quiet, but I knew that couldn't be Earls Colne, which has a grass runway. I decided to call London Stansted, whose radio frequency I had noted on my knee board, just in case of emergencies. I informed them that I was attempting to travel to Earls Colne, but now realised I must have passed it, and could now see a hard runway ahead of me. They recommended that I call up RAF Wattisham, which was probably what I could see in the distance.

RAF Wattisham, during the cold war years, was a frontline fighter base. Latterly it became a base for Army Air Corps helicopters, and a REME establishment for repair and maintenance of rotary aircraft. Now armed with their approach radio frequency, I called up RAF Wattisham.

The friendly ATC replied and said to me, 'I wondered when you were going to call up, I have been watching you approach on our radar.'

By now I was feeling somewhat embarrassed, because I had obviously flown over or nearby Earls Colne and not seen the airfield. After apologising for my incursion into Wattisham airspace, I explained that I had left Rochester for a visit to Earls Colne.

He said, 'That is no problem.'

He then gave me a heading that would take me back towards EGSR. He assured me again, that this was no trouble to him. He was glad of something to do in his control tower, as the day had been very quiet.

Immediately I altered my course for Earls Colne. After I had flown along my new course for another few minutes, the friendly ATC gave me a further heading to fly on, with which I duly complied.

RADAR, the acronym stands for radio detection and ranging, is an amazing piece of kit widely in use in all sorts of applications at sea, on land and in the air, enabling someone to see from far afield what is approaching and at what speed. It has a long history but began to be developed seriously and in great secrecy simultaneously in several countries between 1934 and 1939. Development and refinement of RADAR by British engineers during the war years made it the remarkable aid to navigation and national defence which it is today

The ATC continued to follow my progress on his screen, and moments later said, 'Earls Colne is around five miles in front of you. Can you see it?'

I scanned my immediate horizon, and unfortunately had to reply, 'Negative, I can't see the field yet.'

As I said before, EGSR is in the middle of farm land, interspersed with a myriad of golf courses.

'No problem,' he said, and gave me yet another heading, which was putting me on a direct route to final approach.

After a minute or two, 'Bingo!' I thought, 'I can see the runway.'

I called the ATC at Wattisham and confirmed, 'Golf Zulu Victor has the field in sight, I'll now call Earls Colne. Thanks for your help. My apologies for straying into your air space.'

He responded immediately, 'Are you sure you have the field in sight?'

I confirmed, and thanked him once more.

'Absolutely no trouble at all,' he assured me. 'Enjoy your visit, and have a safe journey back to Rochester.'

I called traffic control at EGSR and was soon descending on final approach, and then it was obvious how I had missed it. There was nothing for miles around other than almost flat fields edged with low hedges, and only a low radiused hangar at one end, with a small office-cum-club-house beside it. I landed on the grass runway, parked next to the few other light aircraft, and walked to the office to pay my landing fee.

After a coffee and a chat with the staff in the office, I had a walk around the airfield and took a peek inside the hangar. To my surprise, there were a couple of guys inside, working on the restoration of a Spitfire. They really are quite a size when you get up close and personal – the Spitfire I mean, not the two guys.

I walked back to my Cessna 172, G AZZV, and carried out pre-flight checks. The airfield was by then closed, so I made blind calls on the EGSR frequency and taxied to the hold for departure. After take-off, I was soon climbing out over those lush green fields, and very quickly lost sight of the airfield. I tried to memorise the topography for my next visit to Earls Colne.

My flight back to Rochester was without incident, and at no point was I 'temporarily unsure of my position', which sounds considerably better than 'lost'. I arrived back at EGTO (Rochester) at 19:25, shut Zulu Victor down, tied the weights to the wings to prevent a gust of strong wind from moving the aeroplane, and made my way back to my car.

Later I recorded my visit to EGSR in my pilot's log book. This trip took one hour from Rochester to Earls Colne. I am pleased to say the flight there on my second visit took only thirty minutes.

Busy Years – 1997 to 1999

During the rest of 1997, through to early May of 1999, my flying hours were building up prodigiously, visiting the airfields at Shoreham, Elstree, Southend, Stapleford, Dieppe, Bembridge, Lydd and Biggin Hill several times.

On one occasion I flew to London Elstree Aerodrome to meet one of my favourite clients for lunch. David Wilson worked nearby at the GEC Marconi Research Centre for Defence Software in Borehamwood. I left Headcorn as usual, and climbed away from the field heading towards the Dartford Crossing. The next waypoint is just south of Stapleford Aerodrome, and when around five miles from Stapleford I called up Thames Radar, informing them of my intended route and destination.

To my surprise, Thames informed me that I would have to take a bit of a detour from the usual route, which is directly overhead the Elstree Studios where the EastEnders set is located. I was informed that Her Majesty the Queen was visiting the studios and the set on that day. The secret service organisation that takes care of royal security on visits had insisted that no light aircraft were to be permitted to fly overhead the immediate area that day. I was also informed there may be armed personnel on the ground.

Obviously, not wanting to be shot out of the sky, I agreed to comply with the instruction. In pilot speak, the reply is 'wilco', abbreviation for 'will comply with request'. In order to comply, on approach to the area where the studios are, I made a wide dog-legged detour, and eventually picked up my original track.

As I flew near the Elstree Studios, I briefly wondered if Her Majesty had looked up, and wondered why all these light aircraft were flying such a strangely circuitous route.

The usual approach to Elstree is somewhat reminiscent of the approach to Kai Tak in Hong Kong, where the jumbo jets fly at an eye-popping low level, apparently flying between blocks of apartments, before turning a steep right-hand banking turn, finally dropping on to the runway, just beyond the perimeter chain-link fencing.

Elstree wasn't quite as dramatic, but you do have to fly quite close to the roofs of two blocks of flats, pulling the power off. When you are safely past, then picking up the power again on short finals, to lift the plane over a row of trees. Once over those, the power comes off again, allowing you to flare out over the numbers, and rapidly lose speed on the uphill westerly runway.

Dave sadly is no longer with us. Stan and I had a wonderful time with him in Florence some years later, watching a local football derby game between Fiorentina and Livorno.

On this trip to Elstree, Dave and I went to a pleasant restaurant and had a relaxed lunch, with serious conversation putting the world to rights and plenty of laughs as usual.

The airspace above the studios was still prohibited so I returned to Headcorn via a reciprocal route.

I said at the start of this chapter that I was putting in plenty of hours flying, and inevitably got a bit itchy to find some different destinations.

Mainly, I was flying a Robin DR400 180 at that time, call sign G TUKE, which happened to be owned by James Tuke, the owner of a helicopter flying school at Headcorn, Thurston Helicopters. He rented out G TUKE by the hour to PPLs. I spoke to Elly and asked her to recommend another good place to take clients for lunch, to create a good impression. She recommended Ostend in Belgium.

So, with this in mind, I studied the chart and planned my route, which would take me from Headcorn to Lydd, then across the English Channel.

Instead of a right turn to Le Touquet a left turn is taken and the flight continues overhead Calais, then Dunkerque, and into Belgian airspace, passing a military base inland, which would have been copied into my flight plan, and over the coastal town of Koksijde, pronounced '*Koksee*' when talking to Ostend approach.

Our client was a senior mechanical project manager, with whom we had worked on several major projects in J Sainsbury stores, across the UK.

I filed my flight plan on the morning of the 27th May. I had stowed an uninflated four-man life raft on the seat in the back, beside Stan, just in case the unthinkable happened whilst we were flying over the sea towards France and Belgium. Three on board, we departed Headcorn at 11:10 and I flew the route as described, and am happy to say we did not need to use the life raft.

Our journey progressed nicely, with lots of good-humoured banter all the way. Stan, sitting in the rear seats, was responsible for the in-flight catering, which consisted mainly of passing around the extra strong mints, a particular favourite of mine. Once we were ten or so miles from Ostend, I gave their approach frequency a call, and advised them of our position, followed by the usual information they required, and the number of souls on board.

Their reply detailed the runway in use, wind speed and direction, and finally they told me to report with the field in sight.

Now for those of you who don't know, every airfield or airport will say the same, whether it's a grass runway of seven hundred and fifty metres, or a concrete runway one and a half miles in length, you are told to 'report with the field in sight'.

Stan had heard all the radio exchanges between me and various ATCs, and had heard them say, 'Report with the field in sight.' As we progressed towards Ostend, I saw the airfield in the distance, which was encouraging. My planned route had worked.

I called up Ostend again and told them, 'Golf Kilo Echo has the field in sight, with approximately three miles to run, on a straight-in approach – long finals – to the runway.'

As soon as the words were out of my mouth, Stan was busily scouring the ground below to see if he could see what I could see. The runway.

The reply came from ATC, 'Golf Kilo Echo, cleared to land after the departing Airbus.'

I read back to them, 'Cleared to land after the departing Airbus, Golf Kilo Echo.'

Hearing the word Airbus twice, Stan shouted, 'Airbus! What Airbus?'

I pointed towards the windscreen and said, 'That one!' An A320 Airbus was streaking along the runway, straight in front of us, and climbed away so fast it was soon into treble figures as it gained height.

The expression on Stan's face was priceless, a mixture fear and disbelief at what he had just seen. He then told me that he'd been looking for a grass runway, because Ostend had requested to report with the field in sight. Hearing that a big jet was in the air, just ahead of G TUKE, blew his mind and composure.

It was fantastic on short finals, then flaring out over the numbers on the runway, with nearly two miles of concrete in front of us. As we rolled along, with our speed decreasing, ATC requested that I taxi to the end of the runway and follow the marshaller.

A bright yellow and black striped van was waiting at the end for us. The words '*FOLLOW ME*' were clearly visible on a flashing matrix sign mounted on its roof. We followed him to a general aviation parking area, then shut down and locked up G TUKE.

The three of us then hopped into the waiting crew bus, which took us to the terminal, where we passed through customs. All visiting aircraft crew are checked before leaving the airport. It was quite a special feeling.

Ostend is a uniquely characterful seaside town, with many good restaurants and shops, and a nice harbour to walk around.

We made several more trips to Ostend. On one occasion, we took a project manager from Skanska, Graham Large, who had recently lost his wife. Graham enjoyed the trip, and I like to think the diversion of a day out may have helped in some small way with his grieving process.

I remember the visit with Graham very well. After another enjoyable lunch in Ostend, we took a taxi back to the airport to make our return journey to Headcorn. I filed our flight plan with ATC, and we took the aircrew minibus back to our awaiting aircraft, proudly parked on the apron.

We were scheduled to be the third aircraft to depart that late afternoon, around half past four. First was a Boeing 747 Jumbo, second was an Antonov AN 225 Mriya, which has a maximum take-off weight of 640 tonnes.

Then, five minutes after the Antonov, allowing time for the wake turbulence to dissipate, good old G TUKE buzzed along the runway, lifting off at sixty knots. It felt like flying forever along the length of the runway, until we reached the perimeter of the airfield. We all agreed how funny it must have looked, to anyone watching from the terminal building, as two leviathans took off, followed by a gnat!

Endnote

On 30th July 1995 G TUKE was damaged at Rochester while attempting to take-off, heavily laden and in formation with three other planes of the same type. It had to return to the airfield, where it struck the airport boundary fence and slewed to a halt. The landing gear had collapsed and the port wing was detached.

The plane was repaired and well-used until a further and final disaster occurred at Deanland Airfield, West Sussex, on 7th May 2000. Whilst attempting to take-off, the plane failed to accelerate. The pilot closed the throttle and applied the brakes, despite which the plane overran the runway into a ploughed field. The pilot and passenger were uninjured and managed to escape before the aircraft was destroyed by fire.

9

Into a New Millennium

'Flying is all about making decisions. If ever you find yourself in a situation you are not comfortable with, do something about it. Make a decision; don't hesitate.'

MARGARET BUTLER

Y2K and Guernsey

The year 2000 came, after many months, or maybe years of preparation and huge expenditure by governments, institutions and corporations to ensure that something as relatively trivial as the way in which dates were stored by computers did not result in a glitch which could have far-reaching and disastrous consequences.

Such was the concern about the Y2K bug that President Bill Clinton mentioned it in his State of the Union address in January 1999.

'We need every state and local government, every business, large and small, to work with us to make sure that the Y2K computer bug will be remembered as the last headache of the 20th century, not the first crisis of the 21st century.'

The concern was that the computers which controlled so many aspects of our life, but especially aviation, might fail, resulting in widespread catastrophe in the skies, as midnight 1999 ticked over into the start of the year 2000. Unless the Y2K glitch was fixed it was feared it could have the most calamitous impact on aviation. Erring on the side of caution, many airlines did not operate flights on millennium night.

As company owners, we were bombarded by our clients with messages asking, 'Is your company Y2K compliant?' Fortunately for the human race, all the clever buggers who built the computers and kept the systems running had our backs covered, as it were, and no aircraft dropped out of the sky. As far as I can recall, beer continued to flow and food was abundant in our supermarkets, so a world-wide collective sigh could be heard, and by early January 2000, all the previous anxiety looked somewhat ridiculous.

The flying exploits of yours truly continued into the new millennium much as they had done in 1999, with several summer trips to Shoreham Airport and more visits to Le Touquet. By now it was becoming almost like driving a bus on a regular route. Every time I went there, whether I was with clients, family, or friends, I still felt the same excitement as I had on my first flying visit with Stan and Elly many years before.

* * *

Jumping forward to August 2000, Stan and I had invited a couple of clients for lunch, but this time, we decided that our destination would be somewhere I had never flown to before: Guernsey, one of the Channel Islands.

For this journey, I chose another aircraft type, a Piper PA 32 – 300. The 300 hp engine was by far the most powerful single-engine light aircraft I had flown. G DENI was a monster of a Piper. Although the profile is much the same as the trusty PA 28 -160, or 180 Cadet or Cherokee, that is where the similarity ended. G DENI had a ferocious 300 horsepower unit under the nacelle, with a variable pitch propeller. Like the Seneca III, in which I had flown to Dinard, G DENI had executive-style seating for a total of seven people, including the pilot.

I had an aircraft type check-out with David Hockings, whom I had known for many years. David and I flew out over the Isle of Sheppey, where we ran through the various idiosyncrasies of flying the PA 32, before returning to Rochester where I carried out several touch and goes, in quite challenging cross winds.

At the end of my circuits, as I was taxiing back to the hangar at Rochester, we watched a Cessna 172 on finals for runway 34 approaching almost sideways in the crosswind. We were both impressed with the skill of the pilot in control of that Cessna, as he landed it very gracefully despite the strength and direction of the wind.

David recognised the plane, and said, 'Oh, that's the Flying Vicar.'

After I had shut down the engine of November India, and locked the plane, I walked over to the Flying Vicar, whom by now was tying down his 172. I congratulated him on his skill in carrying out such a textbook landing in crosswind. He was wearing his vicar's dog collar. I mentioned that I was planning to fly to Guernsey soon, and jokingly asked if he could arrange for some good weather for my trip. I soon realised it was probably not the first time he had heard such a request.

With a smile he replied, 'Sadly, I am in sales, not management.'

I thought this response was a classic. I was so pleased to have made his acquaintance; he was such a gracious character, and not at all pious.

* * *

Stan and I met our two guests on the morning of 30th August, and I checked out November India, whilst the three of them had a cup of tea. After embarking and briefing the passengers, we took off from runway 34. We headed out towards Sussex, via Bewl Water near Lamberhurst, and tracked to the Mayfield VOR, then towards Chichester, the Solent and across the Isle of Wight. My last waypoint on the Isle of Wight before I headed towards the Channel Islands was the Needles at the western tip of the island, which were about 4000 feet below us.

Although I was sure I had calculated my route correctly, I referred constantly to the small screen of my Garmin GPS sitting on the dash in front of me. At times, the banter inside the plane ceased. For about twenty minutes after we had lost sight of the Needles all we could see in any direction was sea. The Atlantic Ocean to our right, and the Channel to our left. If I had messed up, I think the next land we encountered would probably have been the Azores, some 1200 miles away!

Flicking my eyes from scanning the horizon through the windscreen, to the so-small screen of my GPS, I suddenly caught a glimpse of a small island on the Garmin, then looking out of the windscreen again, I saw the outline of the Island of Alderney. I quickly pointed this out to my passengers, with all the cool of a jumbo jet pilot. Alderney rapidly increased in size as we flew closer, and then Guernsey came into view.

On approach, I called up the Guernsey ATC on duty who was a friendly and helpful soul. He confirmed he had received my flight plan, and was expecting us. He told me which runway was in use, and the QFE setting. Then he asked me if I had ever visited the island before. I responded in the negative.

He replied, 'I recommend you descend to around a thousand feet and fly along the western side of the island, which will give you and your passengers an excellent view of the cliffs and beaches on that side of the island. As you get towards the southern end of the island, you will see the runway and airport on the top of the cliffs. Use a left base and report finals when you reach us.'

The remainder of the flight was truly spectacular, flying at 1000 feet above the sea, taking in the magnificent Guernsey coast line. I called up when I was established on final approach, and headed straight for the cliff-top tarmac runway, which made for a super-smooth landing. I recorded our landing time on Guernsey as 11:20, some one hour and fifty minutes flying time from Rochester.

We all enjoyed a superb lunch in St Peter Port, the largest town on the island, then took advantage of the ever-improving sunny weather to stroll along the esplanade, past the harbour where the ferries docked, and the pier. We reached the marina, moored to capacity with expensive-looking yachts and cruisers. The day passed too quickly. We took a taxi back to the airport, where I filed our return flight plan, and at 16:45 we took off again. We had enjoyed almost five and a half hours on the island of Guernsey.

The entire return journey back to Rochester in G DENI was through a clear blue sky. We flew at around 140 knots, passing over the Needles again, Goodwood Chichester Airport, Shoreham, then the Mayfield VOR, and landing at 18:20 back at Rochester.

A Taxi and a Delivery Van

Two memorable flights that I couldn't omit from these memoirs were both taken with clients. One was a planned trip to Le Touquet for lunch with a client, who at that time was the project manager on a large site at Whitehall in central London. His company was contracted to carry out the extensive refurbishment of an existing building. The project lasted from the year 2000, until my company eventually pulled off site in August 2004.

I spent most of those four years commuting to London to oversee progress. It felt as if I had a normal job. My usual pattern of work was to manage several smaller projects simultaneously on sites across the whole of the UK.

My client, Graham Turner, was the project manager on the Whitehall refurbishment. I had arranged to meet him at Elstree Aerodrome in Hertfordshire, which was the nearest airfield to his home, and planned to fly direct to Le Touquet from Elstree.

I had filed my flight plan before leaving Rochester, and fired up a Cessna 172, call sign, G AZZV. I had flown Zulu Victor many times, and was comfortable in this dependable aeroplane. I left Rochester around 09:45 (I tend to use the 24-hour clock in most situations) and after another pleasant, uneventful flight overhead the East Enders studio, I landed at Elstree at 10:25. I went to the control tower to pay my landing fee, and Graham was there waiting for me.

I had checked the Met Office weather forecast for my intended route that day, and all seemed quite benign. Graham had never travelled in a light aircraft before, so was really looking forward to the day ahead and a novel experience. We near enough backtracked the route towards Rochester, flew overhead at a safe altitude, and onward to Lydd, where I had planned to coast out over the Channel to Le Touquet.

Another of the many valuable nuggets of advice Margaret Butler gave me, early in my flying training was: 'Les, flying is all about making decisions, if ever you find yourself in a situation you are not comfortable with, do something about it. Make a decision. Don't hesitate.'

That advice was in the back of my mind whenever I took off and headed out over the Channel. On this occasion, we were getting close to mid-Channel, and I could see nothing but a tall bank of thick grey cloud, that seemed to be getting darker the closer we flew towards it. Now I had two choices. The first was to fly into it, and continue the flight in IMC conditions; the second was to make the decision to change the destination for the flight and avoid getting into a situation that could have serious consequences.

I am glad to say I took the latter, and made the decision to abort the trip to Le Touquet. I put Zulu Victor in a rate one turn, with a thirty-degree angle of bank, and headed for Manston Airport, which is located on the cliffs above Ramsgate. We were soon flying in clear skies again, and bright sunlight.

As soon as I had made the decision, I told Graham what I was doing, and apologised, 'I'm sorry, you won't now need your passport, and won't be eating lunch in a French restaurant. We are landing at Manston.'

When I explained the rapid decision-making process that I went through, for the sake of the safety of both of us, he was not at all disappointed. Rather the reverse, he seemed quite relieved that the guy with whom he would normally joke on site really was a serious and competent private pilot.

I called up Manston approach, gave my details and told them I had intended to go to Le Touquet, but due to unfavourable weather, had decided to re-route. I asked them to let the CAA know that my flight plan had now been closed, because I was intending to land in the UK, at Manston.

* * *

Manston Airport has a long and as yet unfinished history, despite closing on 15th May 2014, with the loss of more than a hundred jobs on the airfield, in an area that already suffers from relatively high unemployment.

The closure has been the source of controversy, debate and divided opinion since then. There is a small glimmer of hope that one day it might be re-born as a viable airfield and airport. I for one am keeping my fingers crossed. However, a judicial review of the government's decision to give the go-ahead has been launched and this has put the brakes on the planning proposal to re-open the airport.

Manston with its long runway was used by the big passenger jet operators to carry out pilot training, including training for Concorde pilots. Often, when visiting the Pfizer site in Sandwich, where we worked, I would pull my car off the road to sit and watch a jumbo pilot carrying out circuits and bumps, and also once had the privilege of seeing Concorde there too.

In the 1990s, Manston had been the base for yellow Sea King RAF search and rescue helicopters, however, they were relocated to RAF Wattisham. Concerns were expressed in 2013 by Sir Roger Gale, the member of Parliament for the Thanet North constituency, that Wattisham was too far from the English Channel. 'We were concerned then – and I have been concerned since – that the distancing of the aircraft from the busiest stretch of water in the world might result in delayed response to any serious incident.

Happily, no such disaster has taken place in the intervening years but the fact remains that the Channel bottleneck that is the Straits of Dover is an accident waiting to happen.'

* * *

To return to my story of Graham's Day Out. We took a taxi into Broadstairs, where we had a most enjoyable lunch in a cliff-top hotel, then returned by taxi to Manston for our flight back to Elstree. We departed Manston at quarter to four, and flying via the Thames Crossing landed back at Elstree an hour later. I went into the control tower to pay my landing fee again, and bade farewell to Graham, who said that he'd had a fantastic, unforgettable day.

I then jumped back into G AZZV, and lifted off from the runway at 17:05, landing back at Rochester some forty minutes later. It had been quite a day, with three take-offs and landings. To me it felt a little like being an aerial taxi driver, with multiple stops and starts.

It had been another day I will never forget, not the least because I will never know what might have happened if I had chosen to fly into those dark, foreboding clouds (memories of Southend again!), and attempted to reach Le Touquet. But I do know, because of those wise words imparted to me by Margaret Butler, that I did make a decision, and quickly. Consequently, both Graham and I had a great day out, and both of us arrived home safely to tell the tale.

* * *

In early September 2012, I received a phone call from a friend and scaffolding contractor whom we used, based at Benfleet in Essex. We had known Andy Jackson from the start of his career as a company owner. We frequently had lunch together, usually in our local, the Rising Sun, at Fawkham Green, near Brands Hatch. Andy would call in to see us if he was in the area.

Andy explained that he and a few friends were due to go to Le Touquet in September, however, one of their group of golfers (Peter Simmonds, son of famous stand up comedian since the 60's, Jimmy Jones, AKA Albert Simmonds) was away in America, and was unsure whether he would be back in time to travel with the others by car to France. Andy asked me if it might be possible for me to collect Peter and fly him to Le Touquet, if he did not get back in time to travel with the group. I said I would be delighted to help, and told Andy to let me know if Peter needed transport when the time came.

I received another phone call from Andy, later in the month, explaining that his mate would, as he had suspected, miss the group's departure. I said that's no problem, give me his mobile number, and I'll call him and arrange it all.

I contacted Peter, and introduced myself. Peter said that he had been expecting me to make contact and said that he was grateful for my help, enabling him to meet up with the others in France. We arranged that I would fly to Southend Airport from Rochester, meet Peter there and fly him to Le Touquet.

At Rochester on the morning of 13th September, I filed my flight plan appropriately, covering the entire journey, and giving the direct route I was going to take, and in case of emergencies arising during the flight, suitable emergency alternative destinations were listed. A flight plan is a very important document in aviation. If there is a serious problem, or God forbid, a crash that prevents you from arriving at your destination within forty-five minutes of your predicted time of arrival, standard search and rescue procedures are set in motion. Your route described in the flight plan is used as the spine of a search pattern, which extends a few miles either side of the planned route, to take into account drifting caused by wind blowing you off course. My route after departing Southend was via Canterbury, then Lydd, and across the Channel directly to Le Touquet.

I left Rochester at 13:30, arriving at Southend Airport twenty minutes later. I parked the Robin DR 400-180 HP, call sign G BOGI, next to a good-sized holiday passenger jet. I climbed out of the Robin and I donned my hi-vis vest. It was amusing to look back and observe the juxtaposition of the two aircraft, as I walked to the control tower to pay my landing fee and meet Peter for the first time. He was a cheery, friendly 'Essex man', and like me, not a skinny bloke.

We exchanged the usual niceties. 'Right, let's get going,' I said.

To my surprise, he said, 'Hold on, I've got to get my golf clubs and holdall. They're over there, by the vending machine.'

I turned around and saw one of the biggest golf bags I've ever seen, together with a bag that Burke and Hare could have used to transport the spoils of their crimes to the local dissection theatre.

We were about to leave the tower when one of the airport staff stopped us and said, 'We'll have to scan all that luggage before you leave.'

So, the gargantuan golf bag and holdall went through the scanner on the conveyor, and after the thumbs-up from border security, the two of us walked out to Golf India, with me leading the way in my hi-vis vest, like a mail-order delivery driver.

The closer we were getting to G BOGI, the more I was thinking, 'Are we going to get all of this stuff, and the both of us into the plane and get this machine flying before we run out of runway!'

I slid back the canopy on the aircraft, and it soon became obvious we could not lift this bag full of clubs and get it inside without causing damage. I suggested emptying the clubs out of the bag. I would then slot them in wherever I could behind our seats. This turned out to be the best idea. Next, I managed to squeeze the golf bag on top of the clubs by squashing it down as much as I could. This was followed by Peter's holdall, presumably filled with his golfer's plaid trousers and shirts, and probably matching plaid underpants and socks too.

I had assumed all his kit would have gone out with Andy and the other guys by car. I never thought to allow for this extra weight. We both climbed up on to the wings, being careful only to stand on the abrasive black footholds beside the cockpit. This is the only safe place to step, as the rest of the plane is made from wood covered with Dacron, including the wings. The construction of the fuselage gives the Robin both agility and speed in the air, but it has to be treated with as much respect as an egg.

I remember glancing at Peter, as we sat snugly shoulder to shoulder inside Golf India, just hoping that I hadn't overloaded the aircraft. I started the engine and received clearance from the tower to taxi to the hold Alpha. As we were taxiing away from the terminal building, I wondered if any of the holiday makers waiting for their call to proceed to the departure gate were watching us pull all of those golf clubs from the bag, and slide them into the back of Golf India, along with the luggage. It must have looked like one of those student pranks – how many people can you cram into a telephone box?

About a hundred yards from the Alpha hold I carried out the necessary power checks in the area designated for the purpose. Once these were completed, I called up Southend ATC, 'Golf-Golf India at the hold Alpha, ready for departure.'

'Clearance to line up on runway 24,' came back from ATC.

I pushed the throttle open, just enough for us to make our way to the large white number 24 painted on the pristine black tarmac. Eddie Stobart Group had taken over the airport a couple of years previously, and had invested several millions of pounds in the facilities, including upgrading the runway surface.

Almost as soon as I had stopped on the numbers, ATC called saying, 'Golf-Golf India, cleared for take-off.'

I acknowledged the instruction, and checked, 'Alright, Peter? Then, Le Touquet here we come.'

I pushed the throttle knob fully in, and G BOGI with its cargo of golf clubs, luggage, and two not-so-small blokes started to roll along runway 24. It was at that moment the nagging thought returned, 'I hope this thing is going to fly with both of us, and all this stuff on board.'

To my relief and delight, with the combination of the 180 hp motor under the nacelle, and the super-smooth runway surface, Golf India soon picked up speed. At around sixty knots, I gently pulled back on the sporty little control stick, and we lifted off from the runway, without any effort, and continued a steady climb upwards to 2000 feet, my chosen cruising altitude. I was so grateful for the low-friction surface of the runway that allowed Golf India to gain speed so rapidly. Well done, and thank you, Eddie Stobart.

Climbing away from Southend Airport, I tracked towards the Isle of Sheppey, then on towards Canterbury, where I showed Peter a fine view of the cathedral.

Canterbury Cathedral dates back to the year 597, when it was founded by Augustine. He was the leader of a group of missionaries sent from Rome to convert the Anglo-Saxons to Christianity by Pope Gregory the Great. Peter was greatly impressed by the sight of Canterbury and my commentary from 2000 feet. Like so many passengers I have taken flying, this was his first journey in a light aircraft.

We flew onward, passing overhead Ashford International, the Eurostar railway station on the high-speed line, and the white, horse-collar shaped McArthur Glen retail outlet. From there it is approximately three miles to the VOR at Lydd. I called up Lydd, giving them my location, and informing them I would be coasting out overhead their airfield, en route directly across the English Channel to Le Touquet.

The weather couldn't have been better that day. We had a good view across the sea to the Normandy coast. We turned on to the French coast just east of Le Touquet. Armed with airport and landing information from the ATC, we approached runway 32. The sun was still beating down. Golf India had served us well. Gently touching down on the main wheels first, followed by the nose wheel, we landed. We were given parking instructions from the tower. I complied, brought the aircraft to a halt, did a MAG check (Magnetto is a mechanical generator, that produces high voltage for spark plugs), and shut the engine down, then slid the canopy forward to enable us to disembark from the Robin. Once the canopy was wide open, we were immediately aware of the intensity of the heat of that summer afternoon and the tranquillity of Le Touquet.

Now came the unloading of the plane. I stood on the wing, reached inside Golf India, and extracted the holdall big enough to contain a marquee, the golf bag and all those golf clubs. Peter picked up his belongings, and we made our way to passport control, which in those days amounted to a cursory glance and a grunt from the douane on duty. He seemed largely uninterested in two blokes from Blighty armed with golf paraphernalia.

I accompanied Peter to the café inside the airport; we both needed some cold fluids. Peter rang Andy and his pals to tell them that he had arrived, and to arrange for them to come and collect him. Peter thanked me again, and we shook hands. I wished him a successful golfing break, which I'm sure would also have included imbibing copious amounts of wine and plenty of good food too.

I made my way back to the main terminal building, to file my plan for my return flight back to G BOGI's home airfield, Rochester. I took off at 15:55.

Now that Golf India was empty of luggage, sports equipment, and another substantial male, the take-off roll was considerably shorter than usual. I left from runway 32, heading towards the coastline. Once over the beach by the mouth of the Canche River, which is not used by the public, I allowed myself some fun. At about 700 feet, with the speed increasing rapidly I pulled a very steep turn heading east towards Hardelot. I tracked along the beach in the direction of Boulogne as I climbed up to around 2000 feet before tracking directly towards Lydd.

By mid-Channel I was flying at around 3000 feet. The air was so still. I sat there looking down at the many ships plying their trade up and down the Channel, and thought as I had so many times before, 'Life doesn't get much better than this.'

As much as I like taking passengers flying, I also like to fly on my own. It is a totally different experience being in the air alone. There are no distractions, you do not have to be concerned for the well-being of another person or worry whether they are getting nervous. It's just you, the aeroplane, and whatever you can see from the air.

At 3000 feet above the Channel, in still air, it feels as if you are sitting on a high trapeze, watching the world slowly move beneath you. Life has just gone into slow motion. When you get this feeling, you know you are hooked, and as soon as you land, you will be thinking about when you can fly again to get your next sensory fix.

Descending to 2000 feet, I coasted in just east of Lydd, and flew back to Rochester via the Ashford Outlet, following the M20 and overhead Leeds Castle, before calling up Rochester for joining and landing information.

The return trip from Le Touquet took just forty-five minutes. After shutting down Golf India, I stood for a minute or two looking across the field, enjoying the peace of the early evening and re-played the whole trip again in my mind's eye. It had been a truly memorable day in the life of a private pilot.

Old Sarum, Wiltshire

Old Sarum Airfield is one of the oldest in the country and the best-preserved example of a World War One airfield. Built in 1917, it was known initially as Ford Farm, until it was renamed after the nearby historical landmark, an Iron Age hill fort. For more than a hundred years Old Sarum has played an important role in defending the United Kingdom, and in the development of British aviation and related activities.

From its inception as a Royal Flying Corps training station during World War One, Old Sarum's original flying field has been in continuous use, albeit that now it is a PPR airfield – prior permission required. The airfield and its range of grade-two listed hangars and workshops provide a unique setting for visiting aircraft. Old Sarum is a good base for parachuting, flying training and helicopter operations, much like Headcorn in Kent.

Back in August 2003, I met a client at Rochester for a promised trip to Old Sarum, and lunch in Salisbury. My client had a personal connection to the Wiltshire area. I had planned my route to take us overhead Biggin Hill, then on to the Ockham VOR, then onwards to Odiham and Farnborough. Our destination, Old Sarum, lies a few miles south-west of the Army Aviation Centre Middle Wallop, a major military helicopter base.

This was to be a momentous flight for various reasons. After take-off at around midday, our route took us overhead Biggin Hill, and on to the west, to pass over the white grand stands at Epsom Race Course, then to make contact with the Ockham VOR, just south of the interchange where the M25 meets the A3.

From there, it is a more or less direct westerly track to Old Sarum. However, as I had done during my first trip to Earls Colne, I thought it prudent to enlist the help of the RAF again, for both their convenience and mine. I cannot praise our Royal Air Force enough. They are most obliging when it comes to helping the fraternity of fellow pilots.

I called up Farnborough first, giving them my details and destination. They obliged with lower airspace radar information, then handed me over to RAF Odiham, where three squadrons of Chinook twin-rotor helicopters, forming the UK Chinook Helicopter Force, are based. I called up Odiham, gave them the same information I had given to Farnborough, and told them that our destination was Old Sarum.

They could not have been more helpful, even to the point of instructing two Chinooks, on their way back to base, to stay away whilst G AZZV was passing close to Odiham, to ensure no down-draft turbulence from the two huge discs of rotor energy did not compromise the lift from my wings.

Both my passenger and I felt immensely privileged, hearing all this radio chatter, knowing the 'conflicting traffic' to which they were referring as they communicated with the pilots of the Chinooks was indeed us, in a single-engine Cessna out from Rochester. Once safely past the immediate vicinity of Odiham, we heard the clearance given to the helicopters to join the circuit at Odiham and land.

Odiham ATC then called me back and said, 'Golf Zulu Victor, have you flown to Old Sarum before?'

I replied in the negative. I presume, as AAC Middle Wallop was only a short distance north-east of Old Sarum, he was keen to know that I was on the ground, and out of the military's way as soon as possible. He offered me vectors to the airfield. This makes life so much easier, as Old Sarum would have been almost as hard to find as Earls Colne was on my first visit there. Old Sarum has a grass runway too, and is surrounded by undulating downland. We were soon in sight of the airfield, where I thanked Odiham for their help.

They replied, 'No problem, call us on your return.'

After obtaining joining and landing information from ATC at Old Sarum, we landed on runway 24, and taxied to the visiting aircraft parking area. I paid my landing fee and the ATC called a taxi for us. We took a moment to look at the war memorial beside one of the grade-two listed hangars. It's a stone structure, reminiscent of an altar, with a dedicatory plaque on one face. On top is mounted a sculpted stone bust of an airman wearing a cap, headset and Irvin jacket, representing the Air Observation Post squadrons based there during World War Two, flying Taylor Austers.

The taxi arrived and in no time, we were walking along the main street in Salisbury. I soon found a restaurant for our lunch, close to the cathedral. Low-ceilinged with oak beams and panelled walls, it had character and a menu of traditional English dishes which I thought would suit my client's taste.

After an excellent lunch, when again I had no alcohol, we strolled around the cathedral and its ancient cloisters, surrounded by immaculate landscaped gardens. Salisbury Cathedral, with its exceptionally tall, elegant spire, is the cathedral church of the Diocese of Salisbury. The cathedral is regarded as one of the leading examples of early English Gothic architecture.

Astonishingly, the main structure was completed in just thirty-eight years, between 1220 and 1258. We were told by one of the vergers that the original Jenny wheel, used to haul up huge timbers and architectural stone when the cathedral was under construction, can still be seen within the void of the roof. It was impossible, once the cathedral was built, to dismantle and remove the Jenny wheel, so the mediaeval masons just left it there. I can thoroughly recommend a visit to Salisbury Cathedral, if ever you find yourself nearby.

Eventually our time in Salisbury had to end, so I called a cab to take the two of us back to Old Sarum. On the way back to the airfield, we chatted about what we had seen, and wondered if we would clash with the Chinooks on our return journey to Rochester. I carried out the usual pre-flight checks on Zulu Victor, called up ATC and asked for departure information. On leaving the westerly runway 24 at 16:45, I climbed to around 1500 feet, thanked Old Sarum ATC for their help and hospitality, informing them I would now make contact with Odiham.

Once again, RAF Odiham was most accommodating, and I was soon flying in their air space. This time, it was not Chinooks, but two RAF Harrier fast jet fighters that were not far away. We heard Odiham ATC call up the Harrier pilots to advise them of our approach and proximity to Odiham. They had to keep well away. Flying at above 450 knots, they would cover a lot of distance very quickly. Since Zulu Victor was cruising at about 100 knots, any conflict would certainly have been catastrophic.

Again, we were well cared for by the Royal Air Force. The courtesy and friendly professionalism of the military air traffic controllers is remarkable. Once we were away from Odiham, they wished us a safe journey, and handed us back to Farnborough ATC to continue our return journey to Rochester. I am pleased to say that at no time during the flight did I see any Chinooks, and more so, I didn't see any Harriers bristling with missiles and maybe fantasising about a bit of target practice on a Cessna 172.

What happened next was a real treat for any aviator. As we were heading east towards Biggin Hill, from the Ockham VOR, in the distance our eyes fixed upon the awesome sight of a British Airways Concorde lifting up into the sky and crossing our flight path. It must have been departing on one of its last flights. It was incredible to think I was flying at the same time and in the same airspace as Concorde. The iconic profile was unmistakeable, the late afternoon sun reflecting off the white fuselage. Even though it may have been around ten miles away we were privileged to be sharing the same sky above southern England.

When we landed back at Rochester at 17:50 we had a chat about the flight and the day in the car park, before making our separate ways home. One more unforgettable day in the life of a private pilot.

End Note

On 10th April, 2003, Air France and British Airways both announced they would be retiring their fleet of Concorde aircraft.

Air France made its final flight on 27th June, whilst British Airways retired its fleet on 24th October after a farewell tour.

Concorde had been in service for twenty-seven years, having made its first commercial flight on 21st January, 1976.

A Labrador and a Hare

Exactly a week after my flight to Old Sarum Airfield in Wiltshire, I had another commitment in my diary. This time I planned to take a client to the north, well north of Rochester, to the aerodrome at Beccles in Suffolk. I chose this destination, as it was only a short taxi ride from the delightful coastal town of Southwold, or so I thought.

Beccles Airfield is located in Ellough, about two miles south-east of Beccles village which sits on the bank of the River Waveney in the county of Suffolk.

Built during the Second World War and always known locally as Ellough Airfield, it was intended for use by the USAAF and completed in August 1942. It had the three concrete runway layout typical of many bomber airfields in East Anglia, and was allocated airfield number 132. The airfield was the last to be completed in Suffolk during the war. By then USAAF had no use for the airfield so it was passed briefly to RAF Bomber Command before being operated by Coastal Command from August 1944.

Post-war, it was used as a heliport, servicing the North Sea oil and gas industries. Currently, it operates as a base for private flights and flight training. The flying school based at Ellough offers PPL courses, as well as instrument and night training. It's located in unrestricted airspace on the Norfolk-Suffolk border.

Most of the concrete runways have been broken up or used as the foundations for modern industrial units. Much of the original airfield is now used for a variety of commercial purposes.

Our departure time from Rochester was around 10:20, in a Piper PA 28 – 180 Cherokee, call sign G BRGI. Our route would take us east of Rochester for a short distance before turning north and crossing the Thames Estuary. Then we headed broadly north-east, towards the Essex coastline. I made initial contact with Southend on approach, and informed them of my intended route. Southend ATC was helpful as ever, giving me lower airspace radar information. I continued my flight over Mersea Island. The main feature of the flat landscape is the network of rivers that meander through the clay of Essex and flow into the sea. My route took me past Clacton-on-Sea, a town where the aviator is spoilt for choice – an airport, an airfield and an aero club, none of which I have visited. As I write I am making a mental note to do so before too long.

Next, the two large commercial sea ports of Harwich and Felixstowe came into view, located on the south and north sides of the mouth of the Orwell River. Shortly afterwards I could see the town of Ipswich, about ten miles inland on the banks of the Orwell. Ipswich is one of England's oldest towns, rich in maritime history and an important centre for the wool trade in Tudor times, and one where my company had fulfilled several contracts over the years.

One of the benefits of this route was the fact that flying north, over unfamiliar territory, I had the North Sea to my right, and a clear view of the coastline to my left. This made it easier for me to spot the coastal waypoints I was expecting to see along the route marked on my chart and confirm my position.

Soon after leaving Ipswich, we could see the former USAF air base at Woodbridge, which I have been told had a runway long enough to land the space shuttle, should it experience a problematic re-entry to Earth and not be able to reach its home base in Florida. There was a chain of similar emergency runways across the world.

Aldeburgh was the next waypoint to recognise, verifying we were on the right course. From the air it looked like another town well worth a visit, with its streets running parallel to the shingle beach. It was once home to the composer Benjamin Britten and his partner Peter Pears, and has been the centre of the international Aldeburgh Festival of Arts at nearby Snape Maltings, since 1948. There are still so many great places for a staycation in Blighty.

Just north of Aldeburgh is the town of Leiston and the two Sizewell Nuclear Power Stations, A and B. The airspace directly above them is restricted so we had to make a wide detour around, rather than overfly the complex of sinister-looking, brutalist concrete buildings.

Following the coastline, we passed over Minsmere Nature Reserve. After another thirty miles or so, Southwold came into view, with its lighthouse providing an easily spotted landmark and an important waypoint. Beccles Airfield is only eight miles north-west of Southwold as the Cessna flies and much like Earls Colne is surrounded by fields. However, this time, I did not need the RAF to come to my rescue. Beccles is much more visible from the air. I called up Beccles ATC and asked for joining and landing information.

Invariably, I find that the duty ATCs at rural airfields are friendly and helpful, and this was the case at Beccles. I was given the wind direction and speed and told to land on 27. The approach was straightforward, followed by a gratifyingly smooth touch-down. G BRGI was soon taxiing to the visiting aircraft parking area. When we disembarked Golf India, after exactly one hour flying time, it was good to smell the country air, and feel the warm August sunshine on our faces.

The usual landing fee payment was made to the ATC, then we phoned for a taxi to take us to Southwold. I must now admit, I had not thought much about getting to Southwold once we were on the ground. In that part of Suffolk roads are few, narrow and winding. As a result, I recall the taxi ride was about forty minutes to get to a town eight miles away!

When we eventually arrived in the town, we had a walk around to get a feel for the place and stretch our legs. We noticed Adnams Brewery, which seemed to be the only industry and main employer in the town. This part of Suffolk appears to be exceptionally affluent, and I am sure its residents enjoy an enviable quality of life.

The lighthouse, built in 1890, is an imposing feature near the centre of

Southwold. If you continue along the North Parade beyond the lighthouse, you are walking along a cliff-top path which offers a wonderful view of the sea and the pier. Southwold Pier underwent a major refurbishment in 1999 and was extended in 2002.

North Parade boasts a long row of frequently photographed, brightly-painted beach huts overlooking the beach. The East Anglian Daily Times reports that these are among the most expensive and sought-after beach huts in England, costing up to £150,000 to buy. Some were in use that August day, with families relaxing. Parents were soaking up the sun, or playing with their children on the sandy beach and paddling in the sea.

Momentarily, I wished I had suggested bringing our swimming costumes and towels with us that day so that we could take a dip in the sea. Instead, we found a charming restaurant decorated in beach-hut colours, where we enjoyed fish and chips. Why do they always taste so much better at the seaside?

Afterwards we looked around the centre of the town with its small upmarket shops, restaurants and a quaint, independent hotel. I have not been to Southwold since my flying trip to Beccles, but it is on my list of places to revisit, maybe next time by car, and to stay for a day or two.

Eventually, after another half hour taxi journey, we returned to the airfield to find G BRGI waiting patiently for us on the apron. I informed the ATC we were going to return directly to Rochester, following the coastline as we had on the outward journey. After carrying out the pre-flight checks on the green and white Piper PA 28, we climbed on to the wing, into our seats, plugged in the headsets and secured the harnesses.

With the engine making a reassuring rumble, I called ATC, and asked for departure information for a VFR flight to Rochester. I jotted the information on my knee board. The throttle lever was pushed forward just enough to move Golf India.

The procedure at the start of every flight is to test the brakes. If they should fail at a leisurely 5 mph, it's possible to cut the power and let the aircraft stop due to inertia. This is infinitely better than landing at around 70 mph, then discovering, to your horror, just after you have touched down on the runway that you have no method of stopping.

Once lined up on the numbers on runway 27, with clearance to take-off at my discretion, the throttle was fully advanced to give maximum power. G BRGI was soon gathering speed, through 40, 45, 50, 55 and up to around 60 knots. At this speed, I was about to lift the nose.

We were just about airborne, when I noticed a large black Labrador, sitting at the edge of the runway, probably no more than ten metres from Golf India. I was taken by surprise to see him and thought, 'I must let ATC know immediately, in case the dog runs out in front of another departing aircraft. It could cause an accident.'

I called up on the radio, 'Beccles. Golf India. There is a large black dog near the end of the runway. This is potentially dangerous. I thought I should let you know.'

Their reply came back, 'Golf India, thanks for the call, but don't worry. He lives here, and he likes to sit there and watch the aircraft depart. Safe journey back to Rochester.'

We laughed at this surreal moment, recalling the scene from the iconic 1955 film *The Dambusters* where the dog waits faithfully for his master Guy Gibson, leading 617 squadron, to return after a sortie. Only in England would this happen, and long may it continue.

The return journey south was the reciprocal of our earlier flight to Beccles. However, this time, my passenger had an uninterrupted view of the coastline, and I was looking out to my left, across the North Sea, dotted with container ships.

We touched down at Rochester at about 17:50. It had been another glorious day and still the sun was shining.

* * *

An airfield that I have not mentioned so far is Andrewsfield Aerodrome in Essex. This is a rural airfield due east of Stansted Airport, close to Braintree, and not far from Earls Colne. Andrewsfield is within the Stansted control zone, consequently all visiting aircraft have to maintain a circuit height of 700 feet, instead of the usual 1000 feet that applies at most other general aviation airfields. Andrewsfield is classified as a PPR airfield, which means prior permission required before visiting. I would phone before I left Rochester, to inform them of my intended time of arrival, aircraft type, call sign and how many people would be on board.

The journey there is a pleasant one, and takes in Hanningfield Reservoir, a significant body of water and nature reserve, which is a useful waymark. Water management is important in rural east Essex, where arable farming predominates. It is reputed to be the sunniest county in England and has the lowest precipitation, so the infrastructure to conserve rainfall and irrigate the heavy clay soils of Essex is vital. A chain of many smaller irrigation reservoirs align broadly with the route of the A12 from Brentwood to Ipswich.

What is it about Essex airfields? Once, on a visit to Andrewsfield I did stray a little too far to the west, into the Stansted Transponder Mandatory Zone, which resulted in me having to phone National Air Traffic Control Services at Swanwick, near Southampton, when I had landed at Andrewsfield and explain why I had flown too close to Stansted.

My younger daughter, Kate, and her husband, Shane, lived in Saffron Walden at one time. I had flown to Andrewsfield to meet them there for a cup of Earl Grey and a natter before returning to Rochester.

When I was about to leave Andrewsfield, the ATC told me to watch out for the hare on the runway. I thought she was joking, and asked what she meant. She explained that when aircraft are lined up on the runway for departure, a hare often appears and runs beside the aircraft. I took note of this, still unsure if she was pulling my leg, and walked back to G BOGI.

After pre-flight checks, I lined up on the numbers of the active runway, and then glimpsed something to my right, about ten yards away from the plane. Yes, it was the hare! I couldn't believe my eyes.

No sooner had I applied full power, and Golf India started to accelerate, than the hare also applied full power, and at first was ahead of the plane. After a few seconds I overtook him, but he was not to be beaten. I watched in amazement as he continued running for all he was worth. He must have enjoyed racing against what he perceived as a big noisy bird rolling along the runway before taking flight.

Shortly, we were airborne and climbing rapidly into the cool Essex air, levelling off at 700 feet for the first few miles, then on up to 1500 feet for the remainder of the return flight to Rochester.

* * *

I can still see that hare in my mind's eye, *Lepus europaeus*. Brown hares are surprisingly tall when standing on their hind legs. They are more muscular and have longer hind legs than rabbits, and longer ears. I was not surprised to discover when I checked later, that hares are the fastest land mammals in the British Isles.

These energetic animals are notorious for displaying erratic behaviour in frivolous chases and frenzied boxing during the spring mating season.

Maybe that explains why, in more superstitious times, witches were thought to be able to shapeshift into hares to escape their enemies. Hares were once symbolic of fertility. The chocolate Easter bunny evolved from the pagan myths associated with the magical mad March hare. Last and by no means least, Disney's Bugs Bunny character is said to have been inspired by a hare, not a rabbit.

Although brown hares were once common in East Anglia their numbers have declined sharply since the 1960s. Many rural airfields provide safe refuges for animals and birds that are being squeezed out of their traditional habitats by modern agriculture. It's another compelling argument for preserving our rural airfields. As Joni Mitchell observed:

> *'Don't it always seem to go*
> *That you don't know what you got 'til it's gone*
> *They paved paradise, and put up a parking lot.'*

The Mary Celeste, Alias Gatwick

As we entered the second year of living with the Covid 19 virus, I heard radio news reports, and saw photographs of airports taken by the drones of news organisations. Rank upon rank of aeroplanes were grounded. Millions, if not billions of pounds worth of aircraft are sitting motionless, neatly arrayed on the taxi ways and hard standing areas of British airports. I suppose the curiosity of it all got to me, combined with the likelihood that this situation will never (hopefully never) be repeated.

With this in mind, I contacted my flying club and booked a Cessna 172, G CFIO from 11:00 until 13:00 on the 6th May, hoping for a break in the weather. May 2021 had started cold and very wet and windy. The 6th May dawned fine, sunny and calm; perfect flying weather.

I must admit now that, back in March 2021, before any easing of restrictions, I had emailed Gatwick, and asked if it would be possible to overfly the airport whilst it was relatively inactive. Air Traffic Control (ATC) replied and told me that they cannot pre-arrange this, but if I was to call them up, en route, if the air space was still quiet, they did not see any problem with granting my request.

I took off from Rochester at around 11:30, and flew on a direct route towards Sevenoaks. This track would take me over Knole Park; almost a thousand acres of woodland, open pasture, low scrub and bracken providing cover for the wild herd of fallow and sika deer, and a golf course. Now in the stewardship of the National Trust, Knole House is situated in the centre of Knole Park. Built between 1455 and 1606, it is one of the largest houses in England. It was a magnificent opportunity to appreciate the size and layout of the huge, palatial Jacobean building, set in its gently undulating, lush parkland.

From overhead Sevenoaks, in the distance I could see the complex of buildings that makes up Gatwick Airport. I called up Gatwick tower, gave them my call sign and position, and asked for permission to approach from the north-east of the airfield, and overfly Gatwick.

A reply came from a friendly-sounding but thoroughly professional controller, giving me permission to enter Gatwick airspace, instructing me to approach from the north-east, keeping clear of Redhill airspace, and then to report when turning on to the southerly track to take me over the airfield.

I was elated to receive the permission I was hoping for, but maintained a cool radio manner when confirming their instructions. I had been quite pessimistic prior to the flight, which is not like me. I had thought to myself: 'I very much doubt I'll be allowed to fly over Gatwick and see it all for myself...'

So, with permission granted, I continued on my heading of 250 degrees from Sevenoaks. This took me on a perfect track to intercept the railway line that connects Gatwick to London and the south coast. Once overhead the railway line, I called the control tower and confirmed my position. Gatwick ATC told me to continue following the railway line and informed me that shortly a Boeing Triple 7 Dream Liner, and an Airbus A340, both approaching from the east, would be joining on a long final approach.

From my position on the eastern edge of the airfield, I could see dozens, maybe as many as a hundred aircraft parked in all areas of the sprawling Sussex airfield.

In 2010, the Icelandic volcano Eyjafjallajökull erupted, sending a plume of volcanic ash nine kilometres into the sky. The eruption was relatively small, but its impact was considerable. The northern hemisphere experienced air travel chaos for almost a month as European air travel ground to a standstill. The disruption caused by the Covid pandemic has had a far more devastating and sustained effect on the whole of the aviation travel industry

As I flew south looking down at Gatwick, my emotions were quite mixed. I was so pleased to be able to fly across what is, under normal circumstances, a very busy approach flight path for all types and sizes of jet aircraft. To see the layout of the airfield from the air, at my cruising speed of 110 knots propelled by my single engine, was a privilege. It was a joy to be flying India Oscar on that sunny May morning.

Conversely, it was sad to see all those shiny jets, so neatly parked, sitting there with no prospect of flying anywhere for the foreseeable future. Seeing so much capital investment lying dormant, I reflected on the far-reaching impact of the pandemic; not only on the people who would normally be busy at work on the airfield, drawn from the nearby towns of Crawley and Horsham, but also those employed by the multitude of companies that supply the aviation industry.

I took several photographs of this incredible sight as a record of the experience, and continued heading south. Gatwick ATC called me again and asked me to fly in the direction of Haywards Heath, and orbit the area, to give time for the two approaching aircraft to land.

I orbited the airspace near Haywards Heath, then started to make my way back on the reciprocal heading. As I flew above the railway line again, this time travelling from south to north, at around 1500 feet, I witnessed the two jets on finals make their landings. First was the Triple 7 Dream Liner, elegant and sleek, reflecting the sun from its white fuselage, followed shortly afterwards by the Airbus A340.

By now I was within a couple of miles of the airfield, and as I approached the overhead, I could see the two liners taxiing to their respective hardstands to disembark their passengers, or unload their cargo. I soaked up the sight on the ground at Gatwick again, and was soon to the north, and beginning my return track towards Rochester.

I received two calls in quick succession from ATC, informing me of possible conflicting aircraft, and giving me directions to keep a special look out for them. The Gatwick flight information service was second to none.

Once I was overhead Sevenoaks, I called up ATC, thanked them for their help, and told them I would now change frequency to Rochester 122.255.

The controller wished me a safe onward flight and I continued back into what is very familiar airspace. I've been flying around these skies for the last thirty-two years.

When I landed back at Rochester, I described my flight to the guys in the club building, and Kelvin Carr in the tower. I just had to share the experience and show them my photographs. They had been tracking me too, on their computer screen and showed me the trace of my entire journey including my orbit pattern over Haywards Heath. Yet another golden nugget in the memory bank.

Flying an Icon

Over the years, the words *icon*, and *iconic* have been used to describe places, people, experiences, books, performances and even chocolate bars. The more a word is used, sometimes without any real justification, the less impact it has.

Now, I will take a risk, and suggest something which I believe is truly eligible to be described as iconic: the Supermarine Spitfire. A true icon of British aviation. The Spitfire, in my opinion, is an iconic blend of design and function and deserves the tag. That is my opinion; if you disagree, that is your prerogative.

I had a major milestone birthday in May of 2021, and both of my daughters spoilt me. I am indeed a very lucky man to have two such wonderful girls.

Both girls always say to me: 'Dad, what on earth can we get for your birthday?' At my age, I have more than enough socks, shirts, pants and pullovers so I was thrilled to be given two memorable experiences.

Kate, my younger daughter knows I like a bit of luxury and she chose to give me a fantastic stay in the largest hotel suite in Stratford-upon-Avon. Now I know what life is like for pop stars or A-listers when they are away from home.

My older daughter Claire gave me an envelope, which I opened to reveal a sheet of paper printed with the letterhead of Boultbee Flight Academy. I read the message:

Happy Birthday, Les, you are going for a flight in a TR 9 Spitfire!

My flight in a Mk 9 Training Spitfire had been purchased a year in advance, and was booked for 28th May from Goodwood Chichester aerodrome. I had flown to Goodwood on my qualifying cross-country in 1989. To say I was delighted with the surprise is the understatement of the year.

Claire and her husband, James, whom I always call Jim, had arranged to take the day off work, so that they could join Jean and I at Goodwood on the day of my flight. We all arrived at 09:00 on that memorable Friday, and reported to the hangar where Boultbee Flight Academy is based. I was introduced to Simon, one of the ground crew, and a fellow PPL. Calmly and professionally, he went through all the procedures I would experience prior to and during the flight. He had such a personable way with him, although I had never met him before, it was like meeting up with an old friend whom I hadn't seen for a while.

Jean stood there and watched as I was being issued with my NATO aviation crash helmet, fire resistant overalls, inflatable life jacket – in case we dropped into the Channel for a swim – and a personal locator beacon (PLB) so that I could be found and picked up by the RNLI, or another emergency responder, I suppose.

I must admit that once I had pulled on the flight suit and zipped it up, I did look and feel the part, even at my age. Next came the inflatable life vest; this takes the outfit to the next level. Simon said he would leave me to connect the strap that went between my legs. Friendliness has its limits.

Once the suit, and life vest were donned, next came the NATO helmet, with built-in noise-cancelling headset. Simon showed me the way to roll this on, from my forehead backwards, and he checked the fit. It was another first for me to wear such a sophisticated helmet. Finally came the PLB.

With all of the necessary clothing and equipment issued, and fitted, Simon then explained *Emergency Actions*. In the unlikely event of a major problem with the aircraft, the pilot will tell you 'Emergency Actions.' I won't go through every detail, but none of these actions phased me. Next, I was introduced to John Gowdy, my pilot for the flight and fellow PPL. The three of us walked to the Spitfire Mk TR9, waiting for us on the apron, on the air side of the hangar at Goodwood Chichester aerodrome. This particular aircraft has the call sign G ILDA, and had been used in South Africa for pilot training.

On that sunny May morning, G ILDA looked like an art installation sitting on the pristine concrete, with a Grumman American Harvard just a few metres away. Whilst John got into his front pilot's seat, I climbed the stair access into the rear passenger seat, where Simon first strapped me to the parachute, then strapped me, the parachute, and the life vest to the plane itself.

I now understand what those old Spitfire pilots mean when they say, 'You don't sit in a Spitfire, you wear it.' It really is that sort of feeling, you really do become a part of the airframe, and feel so secure you know in your head all is good.

John went through the usual pre-start checks. The ground crew confirmed there was nothing behind the aircraft, so with that box ticked, we were ready to move.

John said to me, 'Let's make some noise, shall we?' He then called out, 'Clear prop.' The 1600 horse power Rolls Royce Merlin engine roared into life, with just a few puffs of smoke from the exhaust. I knew this was going to be an unforgettable flight.

With me sitting comfortably in the rear passenger seat, and the Merlin engine running smoothly, John advanced the throttle enough to get us moving, then gave the brakes a test. The test successfully completed, we taxied towards the hold for our departure runway.

To achieve a safe passage to the hold, the Spitfire has to progress in a series of zig zag swerves, a bit like a sailing dinghy tacking across a lake. This is because the nose is high at the front, whilst the plane is on the ground, which impedes forward vision. The last thing we wanted was to barrel into the side of a Cessna.

Once at the hold for our runway, John carried out the power checks, then called the tower, informing them we were at the hold, and ready for departure for a VFR (visual flight rules) flight to the east.

With permission granted from the tower, John applied power and G ILDA started to move across the grass. He then applied take-off power, and wow, that felt almost insane, as the speed seemed to pick up so quickly. I could feel my body being pushed into the back of my seat. Within seconds we were airborne, with the undercarriage retracting as we climbed away from the airfield, giving us a more streamlined profile in the air.

We climbed effortlessly up to our cruising height of around 3000 feet in no time at all. The view through the window and canopy on either side was spectacular; the more so, because the sculpted, elliptical wings of the Spitfire, painted in drab camouflage, were part of the view. As we soared through the air above West Sussex, we were soon close to the flight zone of Shoreham airfield. John called the tower, informed them that we were operating in the area, and gave our altitude. This is both a safety measure and a courtesy to the Shoreham ATC.

Onward we flew, at around 240 mph, and were soon coasting out towards the sea over Beachy Head. This is where we turned, and following the line of the cliffs, the Seven Sisters, John commenced some aerobatics, starting with a barrel roll, followed almost immediately by a 360-degree loop, then a straight victory roll. This is where the Spitfire really excels; its agility is remarkable, aerobatics are effortless. The plane did not show any sign of labouring when climbing, or turning; it just went where John Gowdy aimed it. I already had a face-splitting grin and wondered how much wider it would go and how long it would last.

Once back to straight and level flight, John said, 'OK Les, now it's your turn.' He had already demonstrated to me the sensitivity of the controls. He said 'You have control.'

I replied, 'I have control.' So, yours truly was actually flying a training Mk 9 Spitfire. It was almost unbelievable. I started with gradual left and right turns, which were followed by some pretty steep right and left turns. All the time I was flying I was aware that the plane was smooth and graceful in flight, and not the aggressive monster I had imagined it might be.

I managed to maintain our height of 3000 feet quite accurately, only losing or gaining around 100 feet at first, until I became used to either applying a little more back pressure, or a little less back pressure on the controls. The altimeter was in front of me, and slightly to the left, making it easy to monitor, and thereby maintain height. The time I had in the air passed too quickly, but I am sure however much time I had in the air that day it would be over all too soon.

After a while John said, 'I have control now, Les. I am afraid we have to return to the airfield.' On the way back, John repeated all the aerobatic manoeuvres once more. What a treat; it was just incredible.

We joined the circuit over the airfield, and flew out towards the sea, to allow some airspeed to bleed off, before we approached on the downwind leg of the circuit. We were third in the circuit, so we had to keep a close eye on the other aviators in the air, because their aircraft were probably travelling considerably slower than G ILDA.

Once we were established on the final approach section of the circuit, I stopped talking to John; this is the part of flying that requires the most concentration. I am pleased to say the landing was a classic three-pointer. I was suitably impressed and had to congratulate John on his thoroughly smooth and comfortable landing.

Once off the active runway, we slowly taxied back to the apron outside the Boultbee Hangar. The aircraft was turned around, a final magneto check carried out, then the engine shut down. Silence.

Simon arrived at the side of G ILDA, with the steps, so I could exit the plane and climb down safely onto the tarmac. As I did so, I knew I was wearing my Captain Two Voices wide grin. What a fantastic experience it had been, and one I would wholeheartedly recommend. If you enjoy iconic experiences, you will not be disappointed.

Endnote

Designed in the inter-war years, the wartime Spitfire evolved from the seaplanes built by Supermarine Aviation to compete in the Schneider Trophy Air Race. Reginald Joseph Mitchell was the youthful chief designer and engineer at the Supermarine Aviation Works in Southampton who led the team designing and refining the racing seaplanes.

Supermarine won the Schneider Trophy outright for Britain in 1931 after winning the race three times in a row with RJ Mitchell's ever-evolving S series of monoplanes. In 1931 the S6b achieved a speed of 340 miles per hour above the Solent.

RJ Mitchell died of cancer in 1937 but the Supermarine design team continued to modify and improve the performance of the S series aircraft up to and beyond the Battle of Britain. The Spitfire, together with the Hurricane, defended the skies above Britain throughout World War Two. The advanced features of the Spitfire meant that it could be continuously improved, to counter competition from the Luftwaffe fighters. The rest, as they say, is history – the history of a free and democratic Britain.

PPL Privileges Not Available Any More

I had the good fortune on three occasions to experience a flight from the flight deck of the jet in which I was travelling.

The first was a Monarch Airlines Airbus, en route to Tunisia, North Africa. We were going on a holiday to Hammamet in Tunisia. As I recall, it was a night flight and we were sitting in the plane awaiting departure. The captain introduced himself to the passengers and gave the usual safety briefing, then introduced his first officer, who on this flight was Andy Grainger.

As he mentioned the name, the penny suddenly dropped. That Andy G, was the same Andy who had been the chief flying instructor (CFI) with King Air (sold to Cabair), at Biggin Hill, where I had qualified as a PPL. I remembered him telling me that he was going to work for Monarch. I beckoned the cabin attendant over and I told her that I knew Andy G personally and proffered my very official looking CAA PPL licence which I had purchased via one of the flying magazines that I used to read regularly. At that time, the CAA offered PPLs the opportunity to buy, for just a few pounds, an encapsulated official facsimile of their licence so it could be kept in a wallet.

On her return from the flight deck, the attendant said: 'Andy and the captain would be pleased to see you, and will call you up to the flight deck at some time during the flight.'

The average flight time to Tunisia is about three hours. Eventually I was called to the flight deck, where I greeted and thanked the captain, and had a catch-up with Andy, who by then was married to Janey at King Air.

True to their word, I was invited to the flight deck. The weather that night was interesting! To my astonishment and delight, I was enlisted by the flight crew to help observe an active thunder storm a considerable distance ahead of us, and try to detect the source of the lightening. Three of us each had a section of windscreen to monitor, all intently watching for the next flash. As a consequence of the plane approaching the storm, and the electrically charged atmosphere, I had the amazing privilege of witnessing what is known in the trade as *Saint Elmo's Fire*.

St Elmo's Fire is a visual spectacle caused by the electrically charged atmosphere near the plane trying to discharge through the gold screen-heater elements that run vertically through the windscreen of a jet.

The result was lines of zig-zagging bright neon-blue mini-flashes of lightening dancing across the windscreen. I was told by the captain that this was a rare phenomenon which some airline pilots never witness, so I was truly fortunate to witness St Elmo's Fire.

My second experience of travelling on the flight deck, was on a Tri Star, the common name for the Lockheed L-1011 Tri Star wide bodied passenger jet. Once settled into my seat for the flight from Heathrow to Boston Massachusetts, I called one of the cabin crew over to my seat, and again presented my CAA licence, and as before asked if I could visit the flight deck for landing at Boston's Logan Airport – General Edward Logan Lawrence International Airport. A short while later, she returned with my licence, and said the captain will be delighted to welcome me to the flight deck, and that he would call me prior to landing at Logan. I smiled, thanked her, and settled down for the long-haul flight over the north Atlantic, and eagerly anticipating my forthcoming experience.

Now this is where my story takes a strange twist. Fast forward several hours, and approximately an hour out of Boston, I was asked by the cabin attendant to accompany her to the flight deck. She opened the door, and ushered me in. I was greeted courteously but somewhat formally by both the captain and first officer, and I took my position on the jump seat behind the captain.

The captain, suddenly, in a very inquisitive tone, turned and asked: 'What exactly is your role within the CAA?'

I explained that I did not work for the CAA, the card was just my private pilot's licence, supplied by the CAA. I related the story of how I had obtained the laminated licence. I could tell that he had suspected I was an officer with the CAA, carrying out a spot-check of airline pilots, or something like that. Anyway, the licence had had the desired effect of getting me on the flight deck to experience the approach and landing at Logan from the crew's perspective.

The approach over Massachusetts Bay was really amazing; we were gradually reducing altitude, lower and lower, getting closer to the sea below, with runway 33 clearly visible straight ahead. On short finals, the captain, who was training the first officer, instructed him to apply some more power, as we were a little low on approach. I watched as the first officer applied a small amount of power to all three Rolls Royce RB 211 engines. We gently, but surely, rose a little; then the previous power setting was re-engaged, and a very commendable landing followed this minor adjustment. I was on the flight deck all the way to the hard standing allocated to the Tri Star.

Once the plane was shut down, I exited the flight deck with the captain, who was bidding the passengers farewell as I stood beside him. I often wonder who they thought I might be.

The third and final time that I was permitted to visit the flight deck of a commercial passenger jet airliner was on a return trip from South Africa. My wife and I had visited an old friend who had moved to the RSA several years earlier, and lived in an area of Johannesburg called Kempton Park. Frank and Jeanne lived in a lovely house, complete with a swimming pool, which I used throughout our stay. Our holiday included a trip to the Kruger Park for a few days, which I thoroughly recommend to anyone.

When it was time to return to Blighty, Frank and Jeanne drove us to Johannesburg airport – Jan Smuts Airport at the time, now known as O R Tambo International Airport. We were booked to return on a British Airways Jumbo 747 passenger jet. The flight back was around eleven hours, so there was no race to try to gain access to the flight deck. I enjoy all aspects of flying and was able to leave my seat for a while to look out of the window in one of the back doors, near the galley. The size and scale of the continent of Africa is awe inspiring; in all directions, all you can see is desert, and this takes around five hours to fly over.

Later during the flight, once more, I spoke to one of the flight attendants, and asked if I could visit the flight deck for landing, and gave her my PPL licence, my very official looking CAA licence. Once more, the answer came back in the affirmative, and just before we reached Paris, where descent was initiated, I was invited to join the crew on the flight deck. I had done it again.

I made myself comfortable in the jump seat, and started to ask all sorts of questions about the flight, and the forthcoming landing back at Heathrow. There was a third member of the flight crew, who had been in his bunk in a small rest cabin that adjoins the flight deck. He was quite a young man, and full of enthusiasm; well, who wouldn't be, with the view from this office in a 747? We continued our descent over the Channel and over the Kent air space, getting lower and lower as air traffic control directed the approach and landing.

Once we were overhead London, the third, and by the look of it, the most junior member of the flight crew leant over my shoulder and exclaimed, whilst pointing down to the left of the plane, 'My nan lives just down there.'

I have pointed out many places which my passengers have not been able to recognise from 1500 feet. How I was supposed to pick out a single house from around eight thousand feet was beyond me, but I replied, 'Oh, that's nice.'

Eventually we were instructed to make our approach to the westerly runway at Heathrow, the approach to this runway starts around Battersea, then over Kew Gardens and Hounslow.

However, as I looked over the captain's shoulder in the direction of the runway, it was incredible to see that just like a huge piece of cotton wool, a bank of fog was sitting right on the airport, and started about a thousand feet, going right down to the ground. The captain turned around to point this out to me. He confirmed that, since the fog was so thick, this was to be a full category three automatic pilot landing. He said that the autopilot is so precise it was even possible to dial in the number of metres the plane needed to bring itself to a halt, once on the ground. To say I was amazed is an understatement. I sat there watching both the captain and first officer with their hands just following the controls, which were now being operated by the autopilot, including the throttles and trim wheel, which kept spinning to keep this giant in total trim, and at an efficient flying attitude. We sank gracefully from a clear atmosphere into the fog. Suddenly nothing was visible outside the windscreen for what was maybe twenty seconds or so, but seemed much longer. Then, the tarmac was visible, and we flared, nose up, and gently touched down on this part of Middlesex, known as Heathrow Airport.

As we slowed down along the runway, the captain disengaged the autopilot, and told me that this final part of the journey is the most dangerous, because the fog was so thick, and the aircraft are now being driven around by humans; he hoped that all of the other aircrew were following the moving procedures on the ground at Heathrow. Travelling to our hard stand was a very slow process, in order to prevent colliding with another aircraft, or a building. Another amazing and cherished memory.

Endnote

Lockheed's legendary L-1011 TriStar first flew on 16th November 1970 and you'd be forgiven if you thought none were still flying today. In fact, there is just one flying, operated by Northrop Grumman, which is called Stargazer.

This aircraft was originally delivered to Air Canada in 1974 and was modified in 1994 to launch Pegasus rockets for Orbital Sciences. Today it is still used in that role. The Tri Star is capable of carrying 23,000 kilograms to an altitude of 12,800 metres. It is used to air-launch Pegasus rockets. These can put up to 443 kilograms into low Earth orbit.

The last Tri Star flying, Stargazer's name was borrowed from the American television series *Star Trek: The Next Generation.* Captain Jean-Luc Picard had been the commander of the USS Stargazer, prior to taking command of the USS Enterprise.

And Finally

Well, here we are, nearly at the end of my memoirs, recounting over thirty-one years of holding a private pilot's licence. I have described many of my good experiences in previous chapters, and one or two that I would rather not have had, but as they say, you can't make an omelette without breaking some eggs.

Back in 2012 I took my two grandsons Oliver and Toby, who were ten and nine years old, for their first-ever flight in a light aircraft. Jim, my son-in-law, came too. He is usually called James, but the first time I met him I called him Jim, and it has been that way ever since.

I must admit, although I was really pleased to have Jim, Ollie and Toby as my passengers that day, I was also apprehensive and did have some pre-flight nerves. My cargo was beyond precious. I had the responsibility of my older daughter Claire's whole family sitting in the aeroplane I was about to fly.

I double checked everything during my pre-flight checks, so much so that I think the boys must have thought, 'Grandad, are we ever going to take off?' The boys sat in the rear seats of the Robin, G BOGI, whilst Jim was my co-pilot for the trip.

My captain's safety brief required me to say, 'In the unlikely event of a mechanical problem, there is a ring-tab to the front of the canopy that you can pull upwards. This releases the canopy to allow a rapid exit from the plane if we have to make a forced landing in a field.' However, I did not enjoy saying it to them and fortunately, the instructions were not needed.

I remember looking at the runway ahead on final approach, after flying the Leake family above Kent for about an hour, thinking, 'Thank goodness, we are almost back on the ground and the boys will be reunited with Claire.'

Both Ollie and Toby took the entire experience in their stride and thoroughly enjoyed the flight, as did Jim. Well, he said that he did, anyway.

* * *

In May 1996, I flew to Bournemouth with Jean to celebrate my birthday. My destination was Bournemouth Airport, known then as Bournemouth Hurn and formerly RAF Hurn. The route took us first towards Shoreham Airport, then along the coast to Chichester, before heading over the confluence of Southampton Water with the Solent.

From 1500 feet over the Solent, I could see the green of the New Forest stretching ahead of us, and to my right the enormous oil refinery at Fawley on the west bank of Southampton Water. This site holds many good memories for me. I worked as a lagger at Esso Fawley during 1967 and 1968. An industrial complex like this requires continual maintenance. I have always enjoyed working in massive factories and giant processing plants.

Fawley is the biggest and the oldest of the six refineries currently operational in the UK. The plant was acquired by Esso in 1925 and the complex was rebuilt and expanded in 1951. Owned and operated by Esso Petroleum, the Fawley facility processes 270,000 barrels of crude a day. This equates to one-fifth of Britain's total petro-chemical refining capacity.

The next landmark is Hengistbury Head. The northern side of the sandstone headland tails down to the sea, from which extends a distinctive, hook-shaped spit and sand bar that almost closes Christchurch harbour. The whole area is a coastal nature reserve and a scheduled ancient monument. Archaeologists have found evidence of human occupation from the late Stone Age, which continues into the present day. Three hundred pastel-coloured privately owned beach huts are located on Mudeford Spit. Like those at Southwold, they are highly desirable and priced accordingly.

This was the point where I turned inland to Bournemouth Airport. I landed and was instructed to taxi to the visitor area, where I parked G TUKE next to a Douglas DC3 Dakota. This particular DC3 was owned and operated by a company that specialised in taking passengers for short joy rides from regional airports or military airfields during air shows. I always enjoy the juxtaposition of parking my single-engine plane beside a much larger aircraft – it looks slightly absurd, like a Yorkshire Terrier trotting along beside a Great Dane.

The Douglas Dakota DC3 was produced between 1936 and 1950. Low wing and propeller driven, with two radial engines, it was fast and comfortable. Significantly, it was the first passenger aircraft that operated profitably without the subsidy that came from carrying mail.

* * *

Holding a private pilot's licence has added an extra dimension to my life, and provided me with wonderful opportunities to share experiences with other people, as long as they are not terrified of flying.

From the air, observing colours and patterns in the landscape as the seasons change is a constant source of delight. Buildings, rivers, roads and railways which are often only partially visible from the ground can be fully appreciated when seen from above. Then there is the joy of watching people and animals living their lives, oblivious that they are observed from the little plane above them.

Early one summer evening, over Romney Marsh I witnessed a sheep dog earning his keep by moving his master's flock of Romneys from one field, through a narrow gate, and into another pasture. They were still wearing their winter coats and not moving quickly. The sheepdog was running behind them, darting left and right to keep them moving forward as a flock. The shadow of the plane on the pasture ran just ahead of me.

One of the most spectacular sights, when flying at 1500 feet close to London, is the Canary Wharf Tower, Number 1 Canada Square. The tower was the tallest building in Britain when it was completed in 1991. When flying overhead at that height, the pyramidal roof, topped with a constantly flashing light, is only 700 feet below.

Kent is a county of castles, best appreciated at about 1000 feet. The port of Dover is dominated by the magnificent Norman keep surmounting the chalk cliffs. Some parts of Dover Castle are 2000 years old, dating back to Roman times. Other favourites include Rochester and Upnor Castles on the Medway; Deal and Walmer Castles on the coast, and Leeds and Scotney Castles inland, surrounded by their moats, which make them all the easier to spot from the air.

Returning to Rochester one Sunday morning, whilst flying a Cessna 172 at the circuit height, I was surprised by two vintage fighter planes – a Spitfire and a North American Harvard – passing in front of me at great speed. They couldn't have been more than half a mile away. I watched in amazement as, one after the other, they peeled off in a tight turn to land on runway 20 at EGTO.

In August 2002, almost a year after the terrorist attack on the World Trade Centre, which changed aviation forever, I was taking a client to lunch in Le Touquet in the Cougar, G HIRE. As we coasted out overhead Lydd, and were flying over the sea at 3000 feet, I heard a sharp intake of breath to my right.

'Les, quick, look to your nine o'clock, beneath us, your side ...'

I glanced down quickly to see two French Mirage jet fighters streak below us from west to east, in the direction of Dover. Both were bristling with rockets and guns. This was a frequent patrol off the coast and a sign of the times.

I have engaged in several hobbies during my adult life, but none has gone the distance that aviation has, nor given me anywhere near the pleasure and fulfilment. To be a member of the club of aviators, it doesn't matter whether you are flying a venerable Spam Can, or the latest state-of-the-art model from America. The thing that binds all aviators together is the sheer love and thrill of flying. Lining up at the end of a runway, applying full power and pulling back on the controls, leaving the ground and being in control of that plane; defying gravity and being able to see what the birds see is exhilarating.

When I circle over my house and garden from the air, I feel privileged to be able to look down at it from a totally different perspective than when I'm on the ground. I love being free to fly on top of meringue-like cumulus clouds on a sunny day, in dazzlingly bright sunshine, sporadically catching glimpses of the fields below when there is a gap in the cloud. Or when on top of the clouds to descend into the opaque whiteness, which muffles the engine noise, until you drop out of the bottom of the cloud base, and again can see as far as the horizon.

These sensory wonders have never ceased to delight me, even in the familiar air space above Kent, in which I have flown for the last thirty-one years or so. I would love to think that maybe someone will be inspired to take a trial flying lesson as a result of reading this book, and who knows, might end up like me, having some truly wonderful adventures along the way. In addition, I would like to thank my friends and family for reading about my flying exploits, many of whom will, I hope, have very fond memories of sitting next to Captain Two Voices, who during many flights would point out various landmarks and sights of interest from the air. And I know some of my passengers delighted in the view, only to own up, when back on the ground, that they really couldn't see what I was pointing out from the air, but did not want to disappoint me.

I have had much enjoyment from browsing through my log book and photographs, and writing this account of my life at a time when I have been unable to fly. Since March 2020, the people of the United Kingdom have been subjected to various forms of lockdown, due to the cruel Covid-19 pandemic, which, in March 2021 prematurely ended the life of one of our dear friends, Gwyn Frangne-Bowen.

So, let me finish by thanking you for taking the trouble to read *Captain Two Voices* and hope that you have found it interesting, instructive, thought-provoking, but most of all entertaining.

10

Appendices and Glossary

Appendix 1

Airfields, Airports and Aerodromes Visited by Captain Two Voices

County/Country	Airport or Airfield	ICAO Code	IATA Code
Bromley L B	Biggin Hill Airport	EGKB	BQH
Kent	Rochester Airport	EGTO	RCS
	Lashenden Headcorn Airfield	EGKH	none
	Lydd Airport	EGMD	LYX
	Manston Airport*closed 15.0.2014*	EGMH	MSE
Surrey	Farnborough Airport	EGLF	FAB
	Redhill Aerodrome	EGKR	KRH
Hertfordshire	Elstree Aerodrome	EGTR	ETR
Hampshire	Sandown Airport,Isle of Wight	EGHN	none
	Bembridge Airfield,Isle of Wight	EGHJ	BBP
	Bournemouth Airport	EGHH	BOH
Sussex	Chichester Goodwood Aerodrome	EGHR	QUG
	Brighton Shoreham Airport	EGKA	ESH
Essex	Andrewsfield Airport	EGSL	none
	Earls Colne Airfield	EGSR	none
	Southend Airport	EGMC	SEN
	Stapleford Aerodrome	EGSG	none
Suffolk	Beccles Airport	EGSM	none
Wiltshire	Old Sarum Airfield	EGLS	none
Bailiwick of Guernsey, C I	Guernsey Airport	EGJB	GCI
France	Le TouquetCôte d'Opale Airport	LFAT	LTQ
	Dinard – PleurtuitSt Malo Airport	LFRD	DNR
	DieppeSt Aubin Airport	LFAB	DPE
Belgium	OostendeBrugge Airport	EBOS	OST
Hong Kong	Shek Kong Air Base	VHSK	none

ICAO and IATA Codes

ICAO (International Civil Aviation Authority) codes are separate and different from **IATA** (International Air Transport Association) codes.

IATA codes are generally used for airline timetables, reservations, and baggage tags. *For example, the IATA code for London's Heathrow Airport is LHR and its ICAO code is EGLL.*

In general IATA codes are derived from the name of the airport or the city it serves, whilst ICAO codes are distributed by region and country.

ICAO codes are commonly seen by passengers and the general public on flight-tracking services such as FlightAware. Far more aerodromes and airfields have ICAO codes than IATA codes.

The selection of ICAO codes is partly delegated to authorities in each country, whilst IATA codes which have no geographic structure, must be decided centrally by the International Air Transport Association.

Distances in Nautical Miles

Distances travelled during flights described in the text

From		Destination Airfield	Distance	Total Miles
Biggin Hill	to	Chichester Goodwood	50	100
Biggin Hill	to	Bembridge, I O W	67	134
Biggin Hill	to	Dieppe	75	150
Biggin Hill	to	Dinard	220	440
Biggin Hill	to	Le Touquet	75	150
Biggin Hill	to	Lydd	47	94
Biggin Hill	to	Southend	33	66
Headcorn	to	Bournemouth	100	200
Headcorn	to	Oostende Brugge	95	190
Rochester	to	Beccles	90	180
Rochester	to	Guernsey	170	340
Rochester	to	Old Sarum	95	190
Rochester	to	Shoreham	50	100

Appendix 2

Airfields Visited in South-East England

Legend for the Sketch Map, on facing page

	Airport/Airfield number and name	ICAO. code
1	Biggin Hill Airport	EGKB
2	Rochester Airport	EGTO
3	Lashenden Headcorn Airfield	EGKH
4	Lydd Airport	EGMD
6	Farnborough Airport	EGLF
7	Redhill Aerodrome	EGKR
8	Elstree Aerodrome	EGTR
12	Chichester Goodwood Aerodrome	EGHR
13	Brighton Shoreham Airport	EGKA
16	Southend Airport	EGMC
17	Stapleford Aerodrome	EGSG

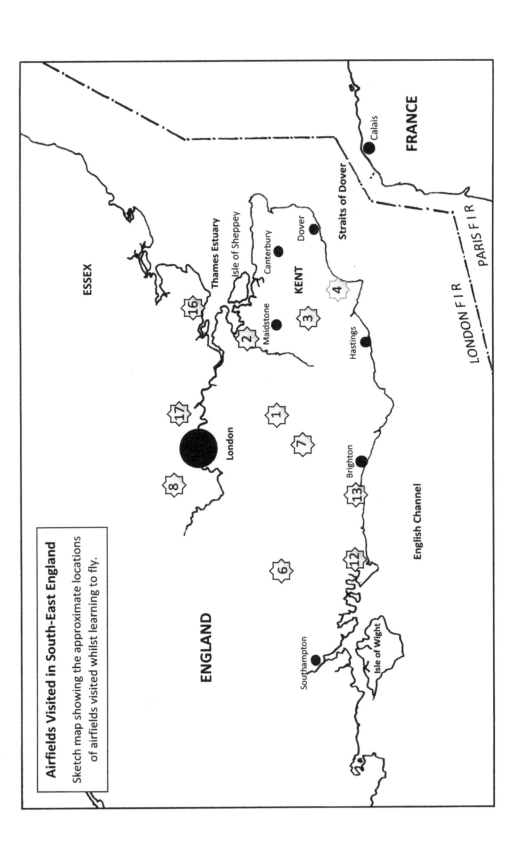

Airfields Visited in South-East England

Sketch map showing the approximate locations of airfields visited whilst learning to fly.

Appendix 3

Airfields Visited Further Afield in UK, France and Belgium

Legend for the sketch map, on facing page

	Airport/Airfield number and name	ICAO code		Airport/Airfield number and name	ICAO code
4	Lydd Airport	EGMD	15	Earls Colne Airfield	EGSR
5	Manston Airport *closed 15.0.2014*	EGMH	18	Beccles Airport	EGSM
6	Farnborough Airport	EGLF	19	Old Sarum Airfield	EGLS
9	Sandown, Isle of Wight	EGHN	20	Guernsey Airport, Channel Islands	EGJB
10	Bembridge, Isle of Wight	EGHJ	21	Le Touquet Côte d'Opale Airport	LFAT
11	Bournemouth Airport	EGHH	22	DieppeSt Aubin Airport	LFAB
14	Andrewsfield Airport	EGSL	23	Oostende Brugge Airport	EBOS

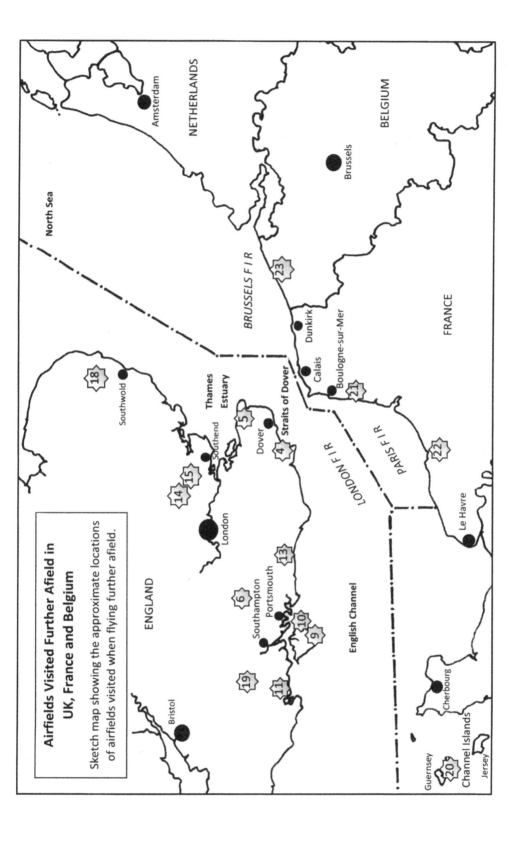

Airfields Visited Further Afield in UK, France and Belgium

Sketch map showing the approximate locations of airfields visited when flying further afield.

Glossary of Abbreviations

AAIB   Air Accident Investigation Board

AI   Attitude Indicator (Artificial Horizon)

AME   Aviation Medical
[Examiner Examines and medically certifies pilots. Each pilot is required to meet specific medical standards for the applicable class of medical certificate.]

ASI   Air Speed Indicator

ATC   Air Traffic Control

CAA   Civil Aviation Authority (United Kingdom)

CFI   Chief Flying Instructor

CSU   Constant Speed Unit or Propeller Governor
[The mechanism which allows a constant speed propeller to work.]

DI   Direction Indicator

ETA   Estimated Time of Arrival

FIR   Flight Information Region

GA   General Aviation

GFT   General Flight Test

ICAO   International Civil Aviation Organisation

IFR   Instrument Flight Rules

ILS   Instrument Landing System

IMC   Instrument Meteorological Conditions

IR   Full Instrument Rating
[Qualification required to be a commercial airline pilot]

MAG   Magnetto is a mechanical generator, that produces high voltage for spark plugs

Mayday   Emergency Distress Call
[Radio message signalling a life-threatening emergency]

METAR   Meteorological Aerodrome
[Report Provides pilots with a snapshot of current weather conditions including wind speed and direction, visibility, cloud cover.]

NFT   Navigation Flight Test

Pan-Pan   Distress Advisory Call
[Message sent in a serious but not yet life threatening situation]

PAPI   Precision Approach Path Indicator

PAR   Precision Approach by Radar

PPL   Private Pilot's Licence

QFC   Qualification Flight Cross-Country

QFE   Pressure Setting for Altimeter, above airfield level

QNH   Pressure Setting for Altimeter, above sea level

RT   Flight Radio Telephony Operator's Licence

RAF   Royal Air Force

TAF   Terminal Aerodrome Forecast, weather report for a specific aerodrome

USAAF   United States of America Air Force

VFR   Visual Flight Rules

VOR   VHF Omni-directional Radio Range

VSI   Vertical Speed Indicator

Lightning Source UK Ltd.
Milton Keynes UK
UKHW050226160822
407355UK00016BA/253